JASON M. BAXTER

The MEDIEVAL MIND
of C. S. LEWIS

HOW GREAT BOOKS
SHAPED A GREAT MIND

Academic
An imprint of InterVarsity Press
Downers Grove, Illinois

InterVarsity Press
P.O. Box 1400, Downers Grove, IL 60515-1426
ivpress.com
email@ivpress.com

InterVarsity Press® is the book-publishing division of InterVarsity Christian Fellowship/USA®,
a movement of students and faculty active on campus at hundreds of universities, colleges, and schools
of nursing in the United States of America, and a member movement of the International Fellowship of
Evangelical Students. For information about local and regional activities, visit intervarsity.org.

Scripture quotations, unless otherwise noted, are from the Holy Bible, Authorized King James Version.

Cover design and image composite: David Fassett
Interior design: Daniel van Loon
Images: C.S. Lewis: © Alpha Historica / Alamy Stock Photo
      Blue grunge texture: © belterz / E+ / Getty Images
      Gold leaf texture: © Katsumi Murouchi / Moment / Getty Images
      Medieval illuminated manuscript: © duncan1890 / DigitalVision Vectors / Getty Images
      night sky watercolor: © Khaneeros / iStock / Getty Images Plus
      flying open books: © LuisPortugal / E+ / Getty Images
      lion: © SEAN GLADWELL / Moment / Getty Images

ISBN 978-1-5140-0164-6 (print)
ISBN 978-1-5140-0165-3 (digital)

Printed in the United States of America ♾

InterVarsity Press is committed to ecological stewardship and to the conservation of natural resources
in all our operations. This book was printed using sustainably sourced paper.

Library of Congress Cataloging-in-Publication Data

Names: Baxter, Jason M., 1981- author.

Title: The medieval mind of C. S. Lewis : how great books shaped a great
    mind / by Jason M. Baxter.

Description: Downers Grove, IL : InterVarsity Press, [2022] | Includes
    bibliographical references and index.

Identifiers: LCCN 2021053195 (print) | LCCN 2021053196 (ebook) | ISBN
    9781514001646 (paperback) | ISBN 9781514001653 (ebook)

Subjects: LCSH: Lewis, C. S. (Clive Staples), 1898-1963—Criticism and
    interpretation. | Literature, Medieval—Influence. | LCGFT: Literary
    criticism.

Classification: LCC PR6023.E926 Z58556 2022 (print) | LCC PR6023.E926
    (ebook) | DDC 823/.912—dc23/eng/20211029

LC record available at https://lccn.loc.gov/2021053195

LC ebook record available at https://lccn.loc.gov/2021053196

P   25   24   23   22   21   20   19   18   17   16   15   14   13   12   11   10   9   8

Y   41   40   39   38   37   36   35   34   33   32   31   30   29   28   27   26   25   24   23

"Without the rich spiritual and literary legacy of the Middle Ages, C. S. Lewis would not have matured into the great apologist, essayist, and fiction writer that he became. Dante scholar Jason Baxter is just the right person to open up that legacy for modern readers and trace how deeply Lewis was shaped not only by the medieval worldview but by the way the medievals thought and felt and interacted with the spiritual and natural world around them."

Louis Markos, professor in English and scholar in residence at Houston Baptist University, author of *On the Shoulders of Hobbits: The Road to Virtue with Tolkien and Lewis*

"Following closely on his well-received works on Dante and on Christian mysticism, Jason Baxter here opens a window onto the bookshelves and study habits of C. S. Lewis, finding rightly that medieval authors have much more profoundly shaped his imagination and theology than most contemporary criticism has noticed. This well-written volume will be of interest both to seasoned scholars and undergraduate students; for the latter it will prove an invaluable introduction to a rich body of great Christian writing."

David Lyle Jeffrey, distinguished senior fellow at Baylor Institute for Studies in Religion

"As the author of *A Beginner's Guide to Dante's* Divine Comedy, Jason M. Baxter is uniquely qualified to guide us through the medieval mind of C. S. Lewis. Those wishing to delve deeper into the ancient roots of Lewis's inspiration and imagination need look no further. Professor Baxter, like Virgil, is a trustworthy guide."

Joseph Pearce, author of *Further Up and Further In: Understanding Narnia* and *Tolkien: Man and Myth*

"I am often lamenting about what our culture has lost. C. S. Lewis is one of our sages who revitalizes the premodern world so that we can again reclaim an enchanted vision of reality. In this book, Jason Baxter offers the church what we've longed for—the tools by which Lewis embodied the medieval worldview—so we too can imitate this forgotten way of seeing."

Jessica Hooten Wilson, Louise Cowan Scholar in Residence at the University of Dallas and author of *Giving the Devil His Due: Demonic Authority in the Fiction of Flannery O'Connor and Fyodor Dostoevsky*

"In this beautifully written book, Jason Baxter invites us to breathe the air of the medieval world that was C. S. Lewis's natural home, providing rich insight into the philosophical and theological imagination that shaped Lewis's thought and writing. But much more, Baxter helps us grasp the urgency Lewis felt to convey the beauty and grandeur of that age to us moderns, who live in a mechanized universe that is robbed of transcendence. This book is a vital resource not only for understanding Lewis and his world but also for making sense of our own."

Gary Selby, professor of ministerial formation, Emmanuel Christian Seminary at Milligan University

"C. S. Lewis described himself as a 'dinosaur'—a member of an otherwise extinct species who could still breathe the air of the Middle Ages and could therefore make it come alive for others. Jason Baxter does a great job of surveying and unpacking this whole side of Lewis's work and its sophisticated, sacramental, and symphonic qualities. The result is a thrilling, moving, and even dangerous ride. Welcome to Jurassic Park!"

Michael Ward, University of Oxford, author of *Planet Narnia: The Seven Heavens in the Imagination of C. S. Lewis*

For my parents, Bob and Pauletta,

and my brother, Josh.

With immortal love.

CONTENTS

ACKNOWLEDGMENTS

I WOULD LIKE TO THANK MY FRIEND Jim Tonkowich for getting this whole project started through his invitation to teach a distance learning course at Wyoming Catholic College. My South Bend friends, Kirk and Maggie Doran, and Steve and Sue Judge, Colum Dever, and Matt Vale provided the original audience for half of this book. Special thanks to Michael Ward and Jahdiel Perez for the invitation to speak at the C. S. Lewis Society in Oxford, where I delivered an early version of the chapter on Lewis and science. Paul Prezzia invited me to St. Gregory's Academy, where I delivered a version of the introduction.

ABBREVIATIONS

DI C. S. Lewis, *The Discarded Image: An Intro-duction to Medieval and Renaissance Literature*, Canto Classics (Cambridge: Cambridge University Press, 1964).

EC C. S. Lewis, *Essay Collection and Other Short Pieces*, edited by Lesley Walmsley (San Francisco: HarperSanFrancisco, 2000).

Letters C. S. Lewis, *The Collected Letters of C. S. Lewis*, edited by Walter Hooper, 3 vols. (San Francisco: HarperSanFrancisco, 2005–2009). Vol. 1: Family Letters: 1905–1931; vol. 2: Books, Broadcasts, and the War: 1931–1949; vol. 3: Narnia, Cambridge, and Joy: 1950–1963. Individual volumes are cited by volume number only.

SBJ C. S. Lewis, *Surprised by Joy* (New York: Harcourt, Brace, and World, 1955).

INTRODUCTION

The LAST DINOSAUR *and the* SURPRISING MODERNITY *of the* MIDDLE AGES

*It is a good rule, after reading a new book, never to allow yourself
another new one till you have read an old one in-between.*

C. S. LEWIS, "ON THE READING OF OLD BOOKS," *EC,* 439

IN THE EARLY 1960s, the editors of the *Christian Century* sent a
question to one hundred of the most famous literary and intellectual
personalities of the day: "What books did most to shape your vocational attitude and your philosophy of life?" The editors were trying
to map the books that had shaped the minds of their generation.
C. S. Lewis was among those polled.[1]

By that time, Lewis had already been famous for two decades, as a
"novelist, essayist, theologian," as the *Christian Century* summed him
up, curiously leaving out something he considered essential to his intellectual identity. He was particularly admired for his *Screwtape
Letters,* his war-years broadcast, *Mere Christianity,* and for his

---

[1]The responses appeared over a number of issues. Lewis's response (along with that of Ann
Landers) appeared in the *Christian Century,* June 6, 1962, 719.

imaginative, fictional writings (especially *The Chronicles of Narnia*, published throughout the 1950s). Already in September 1947, he had been on the cover of *Time* magazine, whose feature article on him was tellingly titled, "Don vs. Devil." And over those years, he had spent two hours a day patiently responding to the letters that poured in from his devoted admirers from across the Anglophone world. He had hosted journalists seeking interviews with him and had accepted dozens of invitations to give lectures and sermons. In sum, his cultural standing was founded on his perceived mastery of psychology, his ability to recast Christianity imaginatively in myth, and for his work in apologetics. As Rowan Williams, summing up fifty years of admiration, put it, Lewis's gift was "what you might call pastoral theology: as an interpreter of people's moral and spiritual crises; as somebody who is a brilliant diagnostician of self-deception."[2]

THE THIRD LEWIS

But there was, as his friend Owen Barfield once said, a third Lewis. In addition to the Christian apologist, whose sagacious words delivered over radio waves had been so comforting during England's darkest hour, and in addition to Lewis the mythmaker, the creator of Narnia and fantastic tales of space travel, there was Lewis the scholar, the Oxford (and later Cambridge) don who spent his days lecturing to students on medieval cosmology and his nights looking up old words in dictionaries.[3] *This* Lewis, as Louis Markos puts it, "was far more a

---

[2]Rowan Williams quoted by Sam Leith, "CS Lewis's Literary Legacy: 'Dodgy and Unpleasant' or 'Exceptionally Good'?," *The Guardian*, November 19, 2013, www.theguardian.com /books/2013/nov/19/cs-lewis-literary-legacy.

[3]It is this "third" Lewis which has emerged especially in recent scholarship. See especially Michael Ward's groundbreaking *Planet Narnia: The Seven Heavens in the Imagination of C. S. Lewis* (Oxford: Oxford University Press, 2010). See also Alister McGrath, *The Intellectual World of C. S. Lewis* (London: Wiley-Blackwell, 2013); Alister McGrath, *C. S. Lewis—A Life: Eccentric Genius, Reluctant Prophet* (Carol Stream, IL: Tyndale House Publishers, 2013); Robert McSwain and Michael Ward, eds., *The Cambridge Companion to C. S. Lewis* (Cambridge: Cambridge University Press, 2010); Chris Armstrong, *Medieval Wisdom for Modern Christians: Finding Authentic Faith in a Forgotten Age with C. S. Lewis* (Grand Rapids, MI: Brazos Press, 2016); Alan Jacobs, *The Narnian: The Life and Imagination of C. S. Lewis* (New York: HarperCollins, 2006). I particularly profited, as well, from *Lewis's List*, cited below.

man of the medieval age than he was of our own."[4] This was the man who read fourteenth-century medieval texts for his spiritual reading, carefully annotating them with pencil;[5] who summed himself up as "chiefly a medievalist"; the philologist, who wrote essays on semantics, metaphors, etymologies, and textual reception;[6] "the distinguished Oxford don and literary critic who packed lecture theatres with his unscripted reflections on English literature";[7] the schoolmaster who fussed at students for not looking up treacherous words in their lexicons; the polyglot pedant who did not translate his quotations from medieval French, German, Italian, or ancient Latin and Greek in his scholarly books; the man who wrote letters to children recommending that they study Latin until they reached the point they could read it fluently without a dictionary; the critic who, single-handedly, saved bizarre, lengthy, untranslated ancient books from obscurity.[8] Before he was famous as a Christian and writer of fantasy, he was famous among his students for his academic lectures, which bore such scintillating titles as "Prolegomena to Medieval Literature" and "Prolegomena to Renaissance Literature." Long "before he ever thought of defending Christianity," he dedicated himself to defending "the beauty

---

[4]Louis Markos, *From Plato to Christ: How Platonic Thought Shaped the Christian Faith* (Downers Grove, IL: InterVarsity Press, 2021), 215.

[5]Armstrong, *Medieval Wisdom*, 39.

[6]For a great description of the sort of late-Romantic philology that excited Lewis, see Alister McGrath's excellent chapter "A Gleam of Divine Truth: The Concept of Myth in Lewis's Thought," in *The Intellectual World*, esp. 55-59.

[7]Alister McGrath, *C. S. Lewis—A Life*, xi.

[8]Lewis read and knew intimately Bernard Silvestris, Alan of Lille, and the *Roman de la Rose*, before any of them had found modern editors, let alone translations. As John Fleming puts it, "Lewis must forever be honoured as a pioneer. Given the fact that the *Roman*, 'as a germinal book. . . ranks second to none except the Bible and the *Consolation of Philosophy*,' its neglect by earlier scholars can be explained only in terms of the work's great length and, at times, excessive strangeness." "Literary Critic," in *Cambridge Companion to C. S. Lewis*, ed. Robert MacSwain and Michael Ward (Cambridge: Cambridge University Press, 2010), 15-28 (17). As for Latin: "Hearty congratulations to Martin on his successes in Latin. Keep it up. To be able to read Latin easily (i.e. without having to translate it mentally as you go along) is an enormous advantage later on. Practice on the Latin *New Testament* where you know the story already and the style is very simple. *Acts* goes especially well in St. Jerome's Latin," "To Anne and Martin Kilmer," August 7, 1957 (*Letters*, 3:873).

and wisdom of the premodern literature of Europe."[9] It was this profes-
sorial Lewis who in a 1955 letter lamented that modern renderings of
old poems made up a "dark conspiracy . . . to convince the modern
barbarian that the poetry of the past was, in its own day, just as mean,
colloquial, and ugly as our own."[10] This was Lewis the antiquarian, who
devoted much—indeed, most—of his life to breathing in the thoughts
and feelings of distant ages, and reconstructing them in his teaching
and writing. We find him recommending to general audiences that
they read one old book for every modern one (as in the epigraph), and
advising those seeking spiritual advice to old books: "I expect I've
mentioned them before: e.g. *The Imitation,* Hilton's *Scale of Perfection,* . . . *Theologica Germanica* . . . Lady Julian, *Revelations of Divine
Love.*"[11] Likewise, we hear him confess, in a 1958 letter to Corbin Scott
Carnell that he could hardly think of any debt he owed to modern
theologians. He thought Carnell had paid him "a wholly undeserved
compliment," assuming his reading was greater than it was. "There are
hardly any such debts at all. . . . Christendom, you see, reached me at
first almost through books I took up not because they were Christian,
but because they were famous as literature. Hence Dante, Spenser,
Milton, the poems of George Herbert . . . were incomparably more
important than any professed theologians." Later, once he had "been
caught by truth in places where I sought only pleasure—came St. Augustine, Hooker, Traherne, Wm Law, *The Imitation,* the *Theologia Germanica.* As for moderns, Tillich and Brunner, I don't know [them] at
all."[12] In sum, this was C. S. Lewis the medievalist.[13]

Even for the editors of *Christian Century,* who summed up Lewis
as a novelist, essayist, and theologian, it was easy to forget that the
man who had become a celebrity Christian had an ardent love for

---

[9]Jacobs, *Narnian,* 165.

[10]*Letters,* 3:649.

[11]As cited in Armstrong, *Medieval Wisdom,* 39.

[12]*Letters,* 3:978. In that letter, he does mention one exception: "Otto's [*The Idea of the Holy*]
I have been deeply influenced by."

[13]See Helen Cooper, "C. S. Lewis as Medievalist," *Linguaculture* 5, no. 2 (2014): 45-57,
https://journal.linguaculture.ro/index.php/home/article/view/48/38.

studying the technical features of medieval language (indeed, sound laws that regulate vowel changes!), manuscript transmission, old books of science, and medieval poetic form.[14] To many of Lewis's readers, it might seem absurd, maybe even irresponsible and escapist, to devote the whole of one's adult life to the study of dead languages (Anglo-Saxon, Old Norse, Provencal, medieval Italian, or Latin) or reconstructing the details of ancient bestiaries (allegorical readings on the spiritual meaning of animals).[15] Sure, studying New Testament Greek is useful, but trying to understand the subtleties of medieval debates, say, on the exact nature of moon spots (as Dante does in *Paradiso* 2)? But Lewis, of course, did do exactly that: he devoted the entirety of his adult life to precisely these kinds of academic pursuits. But perhaps of even greater surprise is the fact that these scholarly pursuits were not separate from his personal life. Lewis did not stop thinking about medieval symbolism, cosmology, and allegory when he left the office. Indeed, what is most telling is that even in the midst of the messy and painful affairs of life and grief and loss, his mind habitually returned to the old books for comfort and consolation. For instance, in an intimate letter to Sheldon Van Auken, after his friend had lost his wife, Lewis's mind could think of nothing better than to recommend his friend read Boethius's *Consolation of Philosophy* in the Loeb edition, with Latin pages facing the English translation. He then followed up with the recommendation of a second medieval book: "As you say in one of your postscripts—your love for Jean must,

---

[14]For good examples of Lewis's delight in the technical aspects of medieval scholarship, see (in addition to *The Allegory of Love*, *The Discarded Image*, and *English Literature in the Sixteenth Century*, all discussed below) "The Alliterative Metre," "What Chaucer Really Did to *Il Filostrato*," "The Fifteenth-Century Heroic Line," and "Metre" in *Selected Literary Essays*, ed. Walter Hooper, Canto Classics (Cambridge: Cambridge University Press, 1969), as well as "The Genesis of a Medieval Book," in *Studies in Medieval and Renaissance Literature*, Canto Classics (Cambridge: Cambridge University Press, 1998), also discussed below.

[15]John Fleming comments, "The professional medievalist must be somewhat bemused by the fact that the literary scholarship and criticism of C.S. Lewis is so little known among his general readership and to some not known at all. After all, teaching literature was Lewis's 'day job' and he expended much energy and talent in writing about it," from "Literary Critic," in *Cambridge Companion*, 15.

in one sense, be 'killed' and 'God must do it.' You'd better read the *Paradiso* hadn't you? Note the moment at which Beatrice turns her eyes away from Dante 'to the eternal Fountain,' and Dante is quite content."[16] Only a few years later, in 1961, when Lewis was suffering from grief over the loss of his own wife, Joy, his mind drifted back to the same passage in Dante. The last line in *A Grief Observed* is the same he had quoted to Van Auken: "I am at peace with God. She smiled, but not at me. *Poi si tornò all'eterna fontana.*"[17]

This is what I mean by the "third Lewis" emerging alongside the first two Lewises we know better, the apologist and imaginative writer. This third Lewis is the writer who spent so much time studying medieval tales and arguments, ancient grammar and vocabulary, premodern rhetoric and the rhythmic flow of ancient speech that he could barely formulate an argument, write a letter, offer a word of consolation, or weave a fictional story of his own without opening up the dam and letting all the old ideas and emotions, stored up in his memory by long reading, break forth. Medieval literature, ancient languages, and the premodern way of looking at the universe were not just Lewis's study or day job, but his passion, his love, his life's work, his spiritual formation, and even his "vocation." In his intellectual autobiography, *Surprised by Joy*, he famously describes three moments in his youth in which he was moved to spiritual longing through reading. He comments, "The reader who finds these three episodes of no interest need read this book no further, for in a sense the central story of my life is about nothing else."[18] The purpose of this book is to explore how this third Lewis is just beneath the surface even in his more appreciated imaginative and devotional writings. We will see that the great medievalist was not a successful modernizer of Christianity and writer of fiction despite the fact that he spent so much time studying old, dusty books, but *because* of them. And this brings us back to the *Christian Century* poll.

---

[16]*Letters*, 3:616.
[17]C. S. Lewis, *A Grief Observed* (San Francisco: HarperSanFrancisco, 1994), 76.
[18]*SBJ*, 17.

Among the ten books Lewis cites as helping shape his sense of vocation and his philosophy of life, there are some we would expect and some we wouldn't. They are George MacDonald's *Phantastes*, G. K. Chesterton's *Everlasting Man*, Virgil's *Aeneid*, George Herbert's *The Temple*, William Wordsworth's *Prelude*, Rudolf Otto's *The Idea of the Holy*, Boethius's *Consolation of Philosophy*, Boswell's *Life of Johnson*, Charles Williams's *Descent into Hell*, and Arthur James Balfour's *Theism and Humanism*.[19] Some of these books, even if they have been largely forgotten by us, make sense in light of Lewis's interest in apologetics. For instance, Arthur James Balfour, a British politician, delivered the Gifford Lectures in 1915, in which he attempted to show, among other things, the limits of a strict naturalist philosophy. In those writings in which Lewis set himself to explaining how materialistic or naturalistic philosophy is incapable of explaining human moral and psychological development, his thought often drifts back to Balfour.[20] George MacDonald's *Phantastes*, as readers of *Surprised by Joy* know, caught the young Lewis by surprise. As a young man, he picked it off a bookstall while waiting for a train, and instantly fell in love with the strange but beautiful imaginary landscape contained within. Lewis's mind was drawn into a foreign world where he breathed the atmosphere of something he had never known before: holiness. Chesterton (or perhaps Charles Williams) is the writer we would, perhaps, most expect to find on a list of those who influenced his "philosophy of life and sense of vocation," as Chesterton, too, was a modern, English writer who engaged a secularized public in a lively, vernacular style. Lewis was a little surprised with himself that he, an atheist at the time, liked Chesterton so much, concluding, "I liked him for his goodness."[21] Lewis adds, "In reading Chesterton, as in reading MacDonald, I did not know what I was letting myself in for. A young man who wishes to remain a sound

---

[19]For more on each of these authors, see David Werther and Susan Werther, eds., *C. S. Lewis's List: The Ten Books that Influenced Him Most* (London: Bloomsbury, 2015).
[20]Lewis commented that *Theism and Humanism* was "a book too little read" (*EC*, 12).
[21]*SBJ*, 191.

Atheist cannot be too careful of his reading. . . . God is, if I may say it, very unscrupulous."[22]

THE LONG MIDDLE AGES

But then we come to other books, older books, books without any obvious connection to modern apologetics or contemporary Christian fiction (to use a loathsome term) and thus more difficult to perceive as having shaped Lewis's sense of vocation. Rudolf Otto was a German Lutheran scholar, whose major work, *The Idea of the Holy*, was a disconcertingly brilliant scholarly attempt to reconstruct the archaic world's experience of the divine, what Otto called the "numinous," the awe-filled and awe-full sense of the transcendent glory of divinity. William Wordsworth's *Prelude* is a two-hundred-page, nineteenth-century poem about a Romantic poet's boyhood awakening to his spiritual and poetic mission. Lewis loved Wordsworth throughout his life, almost as much as Milton, Spenser, and Dante. But in what sense did Wordsworth influence his "sense of vocation"? This seems odd to us. And then we have four even older works: Boswell's *Life of Johnson* (1791); George Herbert's posthumously published book of devotional lyric poems, *The Temple* (1633); then, even more surprisingly, Boethius's *Consolation of Philosophy*, a philosophical treatise written by an imprisoned Roman senator in the 500s AD; and, finally, Virgil's *Aeneid*, an epic poem written in Latin about a mythological hero, Aeneas, who fled Troy to found Rome, written sometime after 31 BC.

In some ways, even if the 1962 list would have puzzled Lewis's fans, devoted to the man for his apologetics or fiction, it would not have surprised his students, or his close friends. The Oxford professor, like most academics, *loved* to make lists, and so enumerations of his favorite authors and books appear everywhere in his writing. His youthful letters to his father, his brother, and closest friends almost always talk about what books he was reading and what he thought his recipients would like about them. Later, at a more mature stage of his career, he

---

[22]*SBJ*, 191.

liked to provide, in his nonfictional essays, lists of recommended authors. In "Religion Without Dogma?," for example, in an attempt to sketch out a traditional understanding of God in the least controversial, broadest terms possible, he refers to accounts one could find in "Bishop Butler and Hooker and Thomas Aquinas and Augustine and St. Paul and Christ and Aristotle and Plato."[23] In "Religion and Science," an imaginary dialogue between author and an agnostic friend, the doubter, exasperated, makes reference to "all those old chaps you're always talking about. . . . I mean Boethius and Augustine and Thomas Aquinas and Dante."[24] In "On the Reading of Old Books," he recounts a list that overlaps with his most famous enumeration of his readings, as found in *Surprised by Joy*. In both places he explains that he read authors "such as Hooker, Herbert, Traherne, Taylor, and Bunyan . . . because they are themselves great English writers." While "others, such as Boethius, St. Augustine, Thomas Aquinas and Dante, because they were 'influences.'" He adds, proudly, "George MacDonald I had found for myself." Unlike modern pedantic scholars who are obsessed with their specialization and, thus, inordinately attach to the periodization of history, Lewis's mind ranged generously over time: "[My authors] are, you will note, a mixed bag, representative of many Churches, climates and ages."[25]

In light of these other lists, the 1962 *Christian Century* one is beginning to come into focus. It includes some of the usual suspects who make their appearance on other lists, lists which indiscriminately mingle Plato and Aristotle with medieval scholastic philosophers and seventeenth-century Anglican theologians. In Lewis's mind, they were all "in league," and made up a cloud of witnesses who belong to what we could call the "Long Middle Ages." Although scholars might wish to define the Middle Ages as the era between 500 and 1500, Lewis felt such boundaries to be arbitrary. Indeed, his whole career was devoted to transgressing these borderlines, as he explained in his 1954

---

[23]"Religion Without Dogma," *EC*, 173.
[24]C. S. Lewis, "Religion and Science," in *God in the Dock: Essays on Theology and Ethics*, ed. Walter Hooper (Grand Rapids, MI: Eerdmans, 1970), 74.
[25]"On the Reading of Old Books," *EC*, 440; cf. "Checkmate," *SBJ*, 212-15.

inaugural address given on assuming a Cambridge professorship
made just for him. He left his beloved Oxford to accept the Chair of
Medieval and Renaissance Literature because he felt the "University
was encouraging my own belief that the barrier between those two
ages has been greatly exaggerated, if indeed it was not largely a figment
of Humanist propaganda. At the very least, I was ready to welcome
any increased flexibility in our conception of history. All lines of de-
marcation between what we call 'periods' should be subject to constant
revision."[26] In the same lecture, he lamented that historians cannot
treat their subjects in the manner of Virginia Woolf, in her modernist,
plotless novels, mingling everything together. "Unhappily we cannot
as historians dispense with periods," and yet, we have to keep in mind
that "all divisions will falsify our material to some extent; the best one
can hope is to choose those which will falsify it least."[27] And elsewhere,
in *The Discarded Image*, Lewis warns his reader that he will use an
ample, encompassing definition of the medieval period: "The reader
will find that I freely illustrate features of the Model which I call 'Medieval' from authors who wrote after the close of the Middle Ages;
from Spenser, Donne or Milton. I do so because, at many points, the
old Model still underlies their work. It was not totally and confidently
abandoned till the end of the seventeenth century."[28] And so, Lewis
has no problem citing ancient Aristotle and Athenian Plato, not to
mention Wordsworth, to help clarify the medieval model. In other
words, it was habitual for him to put ancients in dialogue with Christians, and medieval Christians in dialogue with Romantics, despite the
intervening millennia, in a way that recalled Dante's own blending of
various eras (see his *Inferno* 1, where the pilgrim meets the ancient
poet Virgil). Thus, despite the intervening years and differences in
emotions, Lewis felt them all dedicated to the same project. The real
chasm, the "Great Divide," is what separates "us" (Lewis meant mid-
twentieth-century, machine-using, materialistic modernity), from the

---

[26]C. S. Lewis, "De Descriptione Temporum," in *Selected Literary Essays*, 2.
[27]Lewis, "De Descriptione Temporum," 3.
[28]*DI*, 13.

early nineteenth century. Just as Christians and non-Christians alike will today talk about "light speed" or "inferiority complexes" or the "one percent," without necessarily being advocates of or specialists in Einstein, Freud, or Marx, so too did medieval Christians and ancient pagans share a number of general, "background" beliefs that made them "far more like each other than either was like a modern man."[29] For this reason, Lewis thought an ancient Roman had more in common with human beings from the eighteenth century (like, say, Samuel Johnson), indeed, even with Jane Austen, than either of them have in common with us, "because," he explains, "the old Model still underlies their work."[30] For this reason we can loosely think of Lewis's medieval period as the "Long Middle Ages," which extended from Plato to Samuel Johnson, and sometimes even to Wordsworth.

In addition to this idiosyncratic definition of the medieval period, we find another way in which the third Lewis emerges in the *Christian Century* list—namely, his conviction that ancient books were urgent, not just representative of past beliefs. For the third Lewis, the old books had a sense of *timeliness* (not just timelessness), and thus Boethius and Virgil could share space with a novelist who was his contemporary and friend (Charles Williams). I would like to conclude this introduction by devoting special attention to the presence of Boethius on the *Christian Century* list, for, in a special way, as Chris Armstrong has pointed out, Lewis, as he aged, seems to have increasingly thought of himself as a new, British Boethius. In Lewis's opinion, both he and Boethius lived on the cusps of the Dark Ages, and so, for this reason, the late antique Roman aristocrat could provide a model for his own vocation.[31]

BECOMING BOETHIUS

Boethius, the late antique patrician known as the last of the Romans and the first of the medievals, was born into a wealthy, aristocratic family, and when he was orphaned as a child, he was adopted into a

---

[29]*DI*, 46.
[30]*DI*, 13.
[31]Armstrong, *Medieval Wisdom*, 51-58.

family of even higher prestige. So we should not be shocked by the length of his full name, the indubitable sign of ancient aristocracy: Ancius Manlius Severinus Boethius, adopted by the patrician Symacchus. At any other time, such connections, wealth, and education would have led to venerable and sagacious old age, but Boethius's life overlapped with that of Theodoric, the king of the Ostrogoths who was in the process of taking over the handles of Roman government. And so, in the midst of a time in which the classical world was crumbling, Greek-speaking Boethius felt the need to preserve as much of the classical heritage as possible. He had hoped to translate all of the works of Aristotle from Greek into Latin, then do the same for Plato. He had designs as well to create an introductory textbook for all seven of the liberal arts, and then write a treatise that reconciled theology and the liberal arts, before turning to harmonizing Plato and Aristotle (in a project that anticipated Raphael's *School of Athens* by a thousand years). He was only able to complete a fragment of his project, however, because he was arrested by Theodoric on trumped-up charges of treachery. While waiting for his brutal execution, in exile, he penned *Consolation of Philosophy*, in which he tried to get that project down to its essence while also trying to convince himself that his life had not been a waste.[32]

Lewis loved Boethius. Indeed, he thought that the ability not just to know but to love the *Consolation*, to internalize it, was a mark of which side of the Great Divide your heart was on: "Until about two hundred years ago it would, I think, have been hard to find an educated man in any European country who did not love [the *Consolation*]. To acquire a taste for it is almost to become naturalized in the Middle Ages."[33] In this way, Boethius served as a special exemplar. Just as the sixth-century philosopher lived in an age overrun by

---

[32]For Boethius's struggle to save as much of classical learning as possible in his new age of barbarism, in addition to Lewis's discussion of him in *Discarded Image*, see Henry Chadwick, *Boethius: The Consolations of Music, Logic, Theology, and Philosophy* (Oxford: Oxford University Press, 1990); Antonio Donato, *Boethius' Consolation of Philosophy as a Product of Late Antiquity* (London: Bloomsbury, 2013).
[33]*DI*, 75.

barbarians ("huge, fair-skinned, beer-drinking, boasting thanes"[34]) and desperately gathered and saved whatever fragments he could from the old "high Pagan past," so too did Lewis feel it his duty to save not this or that ancient author, but the general wisdom of the Long Middle Ages, and then vernacularize it for his world, which was now dominated by a new type of barbarian.[35] His own age was one of "Proletarianism," which was now, in a way similar to Boethius's barbarians, cut off from the classical past and proud of its distance from classical antiquity: we are "self-satisfied to a degree perhaps beyond the self-satisfaction of any recorded aristocracy"; we are women and men who have become as "practical as the irrational animals."[36] Having abandoned the study of the old, modern barbarians no longer have access to any values other than those "of modern industrial civilization," and so, Lewis wondered if "we shall not have to re-convert men to real Paganism as a preliminary to converting them to Christianity."[37] In this way, Lewis followed the path of Boethius, who chose not to focus on "what divided him from Virgil, Seneca, Plato, and the old Republican heroes" but rather, "he preferred [a theme] that enabled him to feel how nearly they had been right, to think of them not as 'they' but as 'we.'"[38] Lewis's vocation, like Boethius's, was the humble one of making old books live again: "It has always therefore been one of my main endeavors as a teacher to persuade the young that first-hand knowledge is not only more worth acquiring than second-hand knowledge, but is usually much easier and more

---

[34]*DI*, 79.

[35]See *Letters*, 3:649.

[36]"Modern Man and His Categories of Thought," *EC*, 617-19. For more on Lewis's thoughts on the dangers of a slovenly democracy, see his scathing "Democratic Education," in *Present Concerns* (London: Fount Paperbacks, 1986), 32-36. There Lewis condemns the democratic "hatred of superiority": "There is in all men a tendency . . . to resent the existence of what is stronger, subtler or better than themselves. In uncorrected and brutal men this hardens into an implacable and disinterested hatred of every kind of excellence" (33). And later, "Democracy demands that little men should not take big ones too seriously; it dies when it is full of little men who think they are big themselves" (36).

[37]"Modern Man and His Categories of Thought," *EC*, 619.

[38]*DI*, 79.

delightful to acquire."[39] In light of these concerns, one of Lewis's chief concerns was finding ways to transpose, translate, and re-create the atmosphere of the ancient world in a modern vernacular, as he once explained in a lecture on Christian apologetics: "You must translate every bit of your Theology into the vernacular."[40] In this way, Lewis became a British Boethius, the philosopher whom he once described as the "divine popularizer," who had helped to create "the very *atmosphere* in which the [medieval] world awoke."[41]

Take, for example, Lewis's attempt to make the old Boethian argument on the "wheel of fortune" suitable for a modern palette. During the Covid-19 pandemic, Lewis's "On Living in an Atomic Age" was everywhere on the internet, because, as many commentators pointed out, all you had to do was perform a "find and replace" search (switching "atomic bomb" for "global pandemic") and you had relevant, comforting advice. To the question, "How are we to live in an atomic age?" Lewis replied,

> Why, as you would have lived in the sixteenth century when the plagued visited London almost every year, or as you would have lived in a Viking age when raiders from Scandinavia might land and cut your throat at night. . . . The first action to take is to pull ourselves together. If we are all going to be destroyed by an atomic bomb, let that bomb come when it comes find us doing sensible and human things—praying, working, teaching, reading, listening to music, bathing the children, playing tennis, chatting to our friends over a pint and a game of darts—not huddled together like frightened sheep and thinking about bombs. They may break our bodies (a microbe can do that) but they need not dominate our minds.[42]

---

[39]"On the Reading of Old Books," *EC*, 438.

[40]"Christian Apologetics," *EC*, 155.

[41]C. S. Lewis, *The Allegory of Love* (Oxford: Oxford University Press, 1958), 46 (emphasis added).

[42]C. S. Lewis, "On Living in an Atomic Age," in *Present Concerns*, ed. Walter Hooper (London: Harcourt Brace Jovanovich, 1986), 73-74.

In other words, we should not exaggerate "the novelty of our situation."[43] Nothing has changed. Rather, our new circumstances "remind us forcibly of the sort of world we are living in and which, during the prosperous years before 1914, we were beginning to forget. We have been waked from a pretty dream, and now we can begin to talk about realities."[44]

I love this passage in Lewis, and I found good comfort in it in early 2020, but what interests me the most now is how close it is to the second book of *Consolation of Philosophy*, where Boethius develops a poetic image to describe the world's unpredictable, topsy-turvy nature: the allegorical figure of Lady Fortune, spinning her great wheel, the Wheel of Fortune. In this part of the philosophical dialogue, Lady Philosophy comforts the prisoner, suffering unjust imprisonment and awaiting his brutal execution, by telling him that at least he has awakened to the true nature of reality: "You imagine that fortune's attitude to you has changed; you are wrong. Such was always her way, such is her nature. Instead, all she has done in your case is remain constant to her own inconstancy."[45] No worldly good is ours by possession; worldly goods are always being shifted from here to there, from country to country. In other words, if you take away the allegorical figuration of Fortune, you have Lewis's argument, at some points, word for word. And we know that Lewis *loved* this passage in Boethius. He praised it as the "great apologia" and said it impressed itself "firmly on the imagination of succeeding ages."[46] No one throughout the medieval period who ever read Boethius's allegorized Fortune "could forget her long."[47] It became one of the great commonplaces in the Middle Ages, rewritten and translated continuously over the centuries. Thus, by writing "On Living in an Atomic Age," Lewis

---

[43]Lewis, "On Living in an Atomic Age," *Present Concerns*, 75.

[44]Lewis, "On Living in an Atomic Age," *Present Concerns*, 75.

[45]Boethius, *Consolation of Philosophy* 2.1, in *Theological Tractates, The Consolation of Philosophy*, trans. H. F. Stewart, E. K. Rand, and S. J. Tester, Loeb Classical Library 74 (Cambridge, MA: Harvard University Press, 1973), 177.

[46]*DI*, 81.

[47]*DI*, 82.

did something analogous to the late medieval writers (like Chaucer) who had translated Boethius from Latin into Middle English or French or Italian. He, too, was a "popularizer" of ancient wisdom for a barbarian age. He was following in Boethius's footsteps.

What is more, the professor of medieval literature had *so* much sympathy with the old order and its slow way of life that he felt he spiritually belonged to a generation he had not been born into. He wasn't just a scholar of the Long Middle Ages, but a resident. Through long acquaintance and committed study, Lewis felt himself to have become such a "naturalized" citizen of this distant age. Indeed, he made a bold claim in his Cambridge address, "which sounds arrogant but, I hope, is not really so. I have said that the vast change which separates you from Old Western has been gradual and is not even now complete. Wide as the chasm is, those who are native to different sides of it can still meet; are meeting in this room. . . . I myself belong far more to that Old Western order than to yours."[48] Having claimed, then, that he was more premodern in mind and heart than modern, Lewis went on to explain how this qualified him not only to take on this new professorship, but he could even serve as the specimen to be studied. The quotation is worth citing in full:

> If a live dinosaur dragged its slow length into the laboratory, would we not all look back as we fled? What a chance to know at last how it really moved and looked and smelled and what noises it made! . . . It is my settled conviction that in order to read Old Western literature aright you must suspend most of the responses and unlearn most of the habits you have acquired in reading modern literature. And because this is the *judgement of a native*, I claim that, even if the defence of my conviction is weak, the fact of my conviction is a historical datum to which you should give full weight. That way, where I fail as a critic, I may yet be useful as a specimen. I would even dare to go further. Speaking not only for myself but for all other Old Western men

---

[48]Lewis, "De Descriptione Temporum," 13.

whom you may meet, I would say, use your specimens while you can. There are not going to be many more dinosaurs.[49]

As we can see, Lewis was aware that straining the nerves to understand a medieval poem, written in an ancient dialect now almost forgotten, or studying the regional idiosyncrasies of a fairy romance, or spending months of labor to learn medieval Occitan, seemed absurdly escapist in an age of electricity and mechanized warfare. Can morally serious adults, in an age whose very survival is threatened by economic crises, mechanized warfare, social violence, propaganda, fear, political distrust, and disease, really afford to devote sustained attention to reading the *Roman de la Rose,* in medieval French? What we need are engineers, medical researchers, virologists, and programmers, right? Indeed, the Oxford don gave voice to the objection himself, when his professional vocation seemed most superfluous, in the midst of the World War II. While enemy bombers hovered overhead, and students and professors had to sequester themselves in rooms darkened by blackout curtains at night, could you really justify memorizing "Anglo-Saxon sound laws"?

At first sight this [i.e., academic study] seems to be an odd thing to do during a great war. What is the use of beginning a task which we have so little chance of finishing? Or, even if we ourselves should happen not to be interrupted by death or military service, why should we—indeed how can we—continue to take an interest in these place occupations when the lives of our friends and the liberties of Europe are in the balance?[50]

The answer, from Lewis, of course, was yes, we should. We must, and the clarity of his vision and the forcefulness of his conviction catches us off guard.[51] This book is devoted to exploring *why* Lewis valued such study so much.

---

[49]Lewis, "De Descriptione Temporum," 13-14.
[50]"Learning in War-Time," *EC,* 579.
[51]"Learning in War Time," *EC,* 580.

But for now we need only take note that, given such a lifelong commitment to this course of deep study, we should not be surprised to find medieval phrases, arguments, opinions, metaphors, and images everywhere in Lewis's writing, just beneath the surface. In his popular theology, works of Christian devotion, and imaginative literature, we can find traces of authors from the Long Middle Ages: Plato and Boethius and Dante, as well as stranger and more obscure authors like Macrobius, Calcidius, Bernardus Silvestris, Alan of Lille, Pseudo-Dionysius, and Jean de Meung. Such borrowings from his medieval authors are present even when his writing feels most modern or most personal. This, then, was the third Lewis, the intellectual historian driven by an intense commitment to the old books, to which he clung, stubbornly resisting the rush and pull of the current of modernity. "Translating" them into a modern vernacular, as Boethius had done for classical thought in his own day, constituted his vocation.

CHAPTER ONE

𝒯𝒽𝑒 LOST CATHEDRAL

The Medieval Cosmos

*Characteristically, medieval man ... was an organizer, a codifier,
a man of system. His ideal could not be unfairly summed up ...
"a place for everything, and everything in its (right) place." Three
things are typical of him. First, that small minority of his cathedrals
in which the design of the architect was actually achieved. . . . I am
thinking of a thing like Salisbury. Secondly, the* Summa *of Thomas
Aquinas. And thirdly, the* Divine Comedy *of Dante. In all these alike
we see the tranquil, indefatigable, exultant energy of a passionately
logical mind ordering a huge mass of heterogenous details into unity.
They desire unity and proportion, all the classical virtues, just as
keenly as the Greeks did. But they have a greater and more varied
collection of things to fit in.*

C. S. LEWIS, "IMAGINATION AND THOUGHT IN THE MIDDLE AGES,"
STUDIES IN MEDIEVAL AND RENAISSANCE LITERATURE

IN THE POPULAR IMAGINATION, as Lewis joked more than once,
the term "Middle Ages" evokes a misty blend of knights, castles,
witch trials, torture devices, armor, superstitious peasants (covered
in dirt), and maybe a dragon and princess thrown in to boot. Need it

be said? That was not how Lewis envisioned the time period. Rather, as he pointed out in all of his academic writing, the medieval period was not an age of primitive superstition, but one of bookish sophistication (see epigraph), and anyone who has wandered around a great, Old World cathedral, like Salisbury Cathedral, has some idea of what Lewis's comparison means: it is a paradoxical juxtaposition of astonishing variety, meticulous order, and a saturation of light. On the one hand, both modern and medieval visitors are dazed by the height of the vault, the forest of ordered columns, the infinite variety of decorative motifs and side chapels and stones, while being impressed, at the same time, by the radiation of color, as if light were dwelling in living stones. In a phrase, this is what Lewis meant by "finely ordered multiplicity."[1] But in addition to these structures of literary, logical, and architectural order—the *Comedy, Summa,* and Salisbury Cathedral—Lewis wanted to include one more work of art as "typical" of the medieval achievement: the "medieval synthesis itself, the whole organisation of their theology, science, and history into a single, complex, harmonious mental Model of the Universe."[2] In other words, what Lewis admired most was not simply this or that medieval belief or doctrine, but rather the whole way of viewing the world, the whole ensemble, the whole intellectual "atmosphere" of what I have called the Long Middle Ages, and it was *that* which he, as the modern Boethius, felt it was vital to preserve, explain, and make intelligible, even within modernity. In short, Lewis perceived that for the medieval period, the natural world, like so many stained-glass windows, was, as it were, transparent to a light from beyond this world. What are for us merely natural processes seemed to our ancestors phenomena that pointed beyond themselves. The whole world felt like a cosmic cathedral.

This chapter will build on the previous one by explaining what it was exactly that Lewis saw and felt in the medieval period that

---

[1] *DI*, 11-12. For more on this, consult Bissera Pentcheva's excellent "Hagia Sophia and Multisensory Aesthetic," *Gesta* 50, no. 2 (2011): 93-115.
[2] *DI*, 11.

justified the intensity of his lifelong devotion to the study and "translation" of ideas and texts from the medieval period into the modern
vernacular. And what we'll see is that this ensemble of beliefs that
made up the medieval "model"—Lewis's term for the cosmic imaginary of the medieval period—was not only a kind of work of art, but,
more importantly, an *image*, a powerful thought experiment, a kind
of icon.

It was this medieval view of the universe that became the root metaphor for his "doctrine" of transposition. In one of his greatest sermons,
Lewis develops a musical metaphor, "transposition," to refer to those
various moments when a higher, more complicated system is expressed
in a lower, less complicated one—for example, when a Mahler symphony, with its gargantuan orchestration for four hundred instruments, is transposed for a piano, or when a language with a huge vocabulary is translated into one with a limited one (like Latin into
Anglo-Saxon). This happens, too, in our emotional lives. In the sermon,
Lewis reflects on a passage from Samuel Pepys's diary, in which the
seventeenth-century author, in an effort to describe the delight and
rapture he experienced at a concert, compared that aesthetic experience to the jittery nerves he had suffered when he first fell in love
with his wife, as well as to the jittery nerves he experienced when
seasick! The bodily experience of falling in love, the fluttering of the
diaphragm that we experience when in love, the rapturous shortness
of breath we experience when we listen to Elgar's Cello Concerto, or
the queasy fluttering of the diaphragm we suffer when we are sick at
sea are all, on the mere physiological level, impossible to distinguish.[3]
But if we believe that the emotional life is higher, more varied, and
more subtle than the life of bodily needs and sensations, it follows that
we encounter the bodily language's "limited vocabulary" when the life
of the mind and heart overflow into our physical sensations.[4] Lewis
develops this thought experiment of transposition in order to

---

[3]C. S. Lewis, "Transposition," in *The Weight of Glory: And Other Addresses* (New York:
HarperOne, 1980), 95-97.
[4]Lewis, "Transposition," 99.

construct an explanatory model for how higher spiritual realities are related to lower sensible realities. As my emotions are to my physical sensations, so too is the "higher world" to the natural world of time and nature: it fills this world and makes it seem "too full," "too dense" to *not* point beyond itself.

This, then, is what is at stake when considering Lewis's admiration for medieval cosmology, because for him the medieval universe was not just a system of exploded scientific beliefs, but the natural, icon of transposition, the greatest example of the spiritual world expressing itself in the limited vocabulary of the physical, natural world. And what nuclear reactors, particle accelerators, and the Hubble telescope are for us, the medieval cathedral—and the cosmological "model" it represented—was for the medieval period: a kind of "experiment" that made visible an elusive and deeper truth. It is this iconic vision of the medieval cosmos that Lewis tried to get his students and audiences to see, and feel, and breathe. Thus the Oxford professor's interest in medieval cosmology was not merely an arcane, archaeological antiquarianism. Why? Because being able to see the world with medieval eyes could provide even modern people with a "model" for thinking about the relationship between the natural and spiritual world.

I'll now try to provide a sketch of what that medieval vision was by drawing from Lewis's favorite medieval authorities.

A Snapshot of the Medieval Cosmos

Today, if we read the ancient statesman and author Cicero at all, it is because we think of him as a great exemplar of ancient republican politics, as the orator who defended the republic from tyranny by means of the elegant word. In the Middle Ages, though, Cicero's fame was due to a short, visionary treatise, the "Dream of Scipio," a ten-page account of a Roman general's prophetic dream that served as the concluding chapter to his own attempt to respond to Plato in his own Latin-speaking *Republic*. In the medieval period, the pages that make up this visionary dream tale were copied out independently from the rest of the text, in part because a writer, several centuries later in late antiquity, Macrobius—whose writing is analyzed by Lewis in *Discarded Image*[5]—had made it famous by devoting a three hundred-page commentary to it. Macrobius, a Latin-writing Platonist, was working sometime in the early 400s AD, and he was convinced that every word in Cicero's visionary account had a deep, mystical significance. This belief conditioned the next thousand years to read Cicero's "Dream of Scipio" in hushed, reverent tones, as if, within these pages, the deep mysteries of the universe were revealed to those with eyes to see. Lewis knew these texts intimately.

In Cicero's imaginative account Scipio floats up through the spheres of the heavens and comes to stand at the apex of the universe in order to take in a "view from above." Once there, Scipio (like Dante over a millennium later) is warmly greeted by his male ancestors, who give him lessons in the Roman virtues of honor, justice, and duty. They also make him turn around to contemplate the universe stretched out beneath his feet. At one particularly dramatic moment, Scipio looks down and sees the cosmos moving beneath his feet, and then, hearing an incredible music, he asks, "What is this sound, so loud and yet so sweet, that fills my ears?" His guide answers,

> That is the sound produced by the impetus and momentum of the spheres themselves. It is made up of intervals which, though unequal, are determined systematically by fixed proportions. The blend of high and low notes produces an even flow of various harmonies. . . . By imitating this system with strings and voices experts have succeeded in opening a way back to this place. . . . Filled with this sound, people's ears have become deaf to it.[6]

In other words, the planets are spaced out proportionally to one another, so that the distances between Earth and Mars, and Venus and Jupiter, correspond to harmonic intervals of chords. As the planets rotate, they create a kind of intellectual music, to which we earthlings have become deaf, but

---

[5]*DI*, 60-69.

[6]Cicero, *The Republic and the Laws*, trans. Niall Rudd, Oxford World's Classics (Oxford: Oxford University Press, 1998), 90.

we can regain the ability to hear this music through study or through beautiful music, which imitates the same harmonic proportions.

This idea of a musical universe—whose planets are spaced out like strings on a musical instrument—delighted the imaginations of medieval thinkers. Boethius, to take one example, borrowed this idea from Cicero. In a particularly beautiful poem in his *Consolation of Philosophy*, Boethius, too, imagines himself high above our universe, viewing the cosmos stretched out beneath his feet. You can hear the author's excitement and delight as he describes the choreographed movements of the universe:

> Starmaker, master of spheres,
> At whose command the heavens spin
> In the constellations' dance that you
> On your steady throne have choreographed,
> Bright stars grow dim as you bring on the moon,
> Crescent or gibbous, reflecting her brother's
> Dazzling fire. . . .
> When leaves fall and the cold of winter
> Blows from the north, our days diminish,
> But then, in summer's burgeoning heat
> The dark hours of nighttime dwindle. . . .
> Not even the blowing winds are random,
> But Boreas strips leaves from the trees
> And Zephyrus brings on gentling nurture.[7]

"Not even the blowing winds are random," says Boethius rhapsodically. In other words, Boethius closed his eyes, looked at the earth in his mind's eye, watched its seasons springing up and falling away, and perceived the heavens rotating, all in ordered rhythms. This is what

---

[7]Boethius, *Consolation of Philosophy* 1.5 (18-19). For Boethius's Latin, I use *De Consolatione Philosophiae*, ed. Claudio Moreschini (Berlin: de Gruyter, 2005). For Boethius's poetry, I like *Consolation of Philosophy*, trans. David Slavitt (Cambridge, MA: Harvard University Press, 2008), on account of its lyrical quality. (The translation quoted here is Slavitt's.) But for the prose I prefer the literalism of the old Loeb volume: *Theological Tractates, The Consolation of Philosophy*, trans. H. F. Stewart, E. K. Rand, and S. J. Tester, Loeb Classical Library 74 (Cambridge, MA: Harvard University Press, 1973).

Boethius, in his lesser-known work *De musica*, called "the music of the cosmos." For Boethius, as for Cicero, there is a rational order that keeps the world in balance, keeping it from spinning out of control. It ensures that elements of different kinds bond properly to one another; it regulates how the seasons cycle in an ongoing carousel; this order also regulates how the stars and planets turn. He calls this cosmic order "music" because it is a deep, mathematical harmony that frames out the world in understandable patterns. What is more, Boethius (again like Cicero) taught that through instrumental music we can regain a "taste" of the musicality of the world, and thus retune our souls to cosmic music. Music is philosophical therapy, bringing the soul back into tune with the great Conductor's universe. This is why the *Consolation of Philosophy* alternates between prose and verse.[8]

In a 1956 lecture to the Zoological Laboratory in Cambridge, we find Lewis not only giving a précis of his *Discarded Image* but also trying to "perform" the sound of this symphonic cosmos. In the lecture, he asks his audience of modern scientists to conduct a thought experiment: "Go out on any starry night and walk alone for half an hour, resolutely assuming that the pre-Copernican astronomy is true. Look up at the sky with the assumption in your mind."[9] And if you do so, you will be able to catch a glimpse of how the old universe at once "abashes and exalts the mind,"[10] in contrast to the modern conception of the world, which imposes on the mind a sense of being lost in in-finite and vast space. He explains that if we look up into the sky with medieval expectations in mind, then we will feel it both as finite ("hard, clear, sudden as a national frontier"[11]) but also as pushing down on us ("because the Earth is an absolute center, and Earthwards from any part of this immense universe is downwards, you will find that you are

---

[8]David Chamberlain, "Philosophy of Music in the *Consolatio* of Boethius," *Speculum* 45, no. 1 (1970): 80-97; Stephen Blackwood, *The Consolation of Boethius as Poetic Liturgy* (Oxford: Oxford University Press, 2015).

[9]Lewis, "Imagination and Thought," in *Studies in Medieval and Renaissance Literature*, Canto Classics (Cambridge: Cambridge University Press, 1998), 47.

[10]Lewis, "Imagination and Thought," 48.

[11]Lewis, "Imagination and Thought," 48.

looking at the planets and stars in terms not merely of 'distance' but of the very special kind of distance which we call 'height'"[12]):

> These two factors taken together—enormous but finite size, and distance which, however vast, remain unambiguously vertical, and indeed vertiginous—at once present you with something which differs from the Newtonian picture rather as a great building differs from a great jungle. You can lose yourself in infinity; there is indeed nothing much else you can do with it. It arouses questions, it prompts to a certain kind of wonder and reverie, usually a somber kind. . . . But it answers no questions.[13]

In addition to Macrobius, Lewis also believed that another author was foundational for the medieval model: Calcidius, who wrote, at some point in late antiquity, a massively tedious but extremely successful commentary on Plato's *Timaeus*, the only work of Plato to be read throughout the medieval period. Calcidius crawls passage by passage through Plato's text, dividing the text up into blocks and taking the occasion to provide what he thought would be the necessary background for each subject.[14] In this way, Calcidius, who never says no to a digression, provides a manualistic introduction to any field of medieval science you could hope to know about. He was so digressive that, four hundred pages after he started, he had only made it halfway through the Platonic text he wished to comment on.

But what is a bizarre and tiresome book for us was a treasure for medieval students and scholars. On more than one occasion we find Calcidius a little breathless before his vision. When he looked up at the heavens, he saw "a perfect, unchanging symphony" because the stars "are borne round in a unified and constant movement, adhering to the [the largest sphere which embraces all things] as it leads them round, always maintaining one and the same position and preserving their order in an unvarying pattern, never admitting any change in position,

---

[12]Lewis, "Imagination and Thought," 48.

[13]Lewis, "Imagination and Thought," 48.

[14]Calcidius, *On Plato's Timaeus*, ed. John Magee, Dumbarton Oaks Medieval Library (Cambridge, MA: Harvard University Press, 2014).

ascent, size, or even color."[15] But when he lets his ecstatic eyes drift back down to everything below the moon, like some medieval anticipation of Cormac McCarthy, he is disgusted. This is the realm of "birth and death" and "increase and diminution, every kind of transformation, and transposition form place to place" where "murder, violence, madness" dwell.[16] Lewis poignantly described this medieval attitude by likening the state of human beings to those who watch the celestial spectacle from afar, from the outskirts. Watching *its* beauty, we are overwhelmed, and desire to imitate it to the extent we can. We are, in a word, "anthropoperipheral": "We are creatures of the Margin."[17]

Over his lengthy commentary, Calcidius builds up a picture of the world in his reader's mind: the movement of stars and planets, the interaction of elements, the whole moving picture of the world. But the genius of the vision is found in how all of these movements participate in the same underlying pattern, the deep music or mathematical harmony that rules the world. For Calcidius, "mathematics" is more real than the visible, because it is the rational design of which everything else is merely a physical expression. By perceiving this deep level of numbers, we can discover the mathematical skeleton beneath the world's skin, and so can get at the "real" world, the deep world. We're now beginning to see why the metaphor of cathedral is pertinent to medieval cosmology. For Calcidius, and the rest of the tradition, if you cultivate a perception of the deep harmony of nature, it leads to worship, because the "soul, fashioned after the same pattern as the celestial bodies, immediately recognizes its own natural affinity to them."[18] In other words, despite the messiness of earthly reality, we find underneath the material a paradigm of order, and thus we can see that, in an extraordinary phrase, "time is an *image* of eternity."[19] Even more significantly, these harmonic patterns are likened to the longing and groans of a world that is earnestly engaged in making itself as like the eternal

---

[15]Calcidius, *On Plato's Timaeus*, 231.
[16]Calcidius, *On Plato's Timaeus*, 243.
[17]*DI*, 58.
[18]Calcidius, *On Plato's Timaeus*, 211.
[19]Calcidius, *On Plato's Timaeus*, 157; repeated in Boethius.

simplicity of the divine as it can. Eternity is the world's "paradigm" (its exemplar, goal, and end), and that end is invisible and full of joy, the realm of "pure intelligible light." For this reason, the visible world, in Plato's phrase, is a great "icon": it is an artistic representation that translates into a new medium the eternal principles of a higher order. The very physical movements of the world constitute a kind of longing to measure up. Physics is prayer in an iconic universe.[20] Thus the universe is a kind of text, which inspires contemplation of the deep patterns built in by the craftsman.[21] All of these orchestrated motions exist because they constitute the best possible way to make manifest the perfection of eternity.[22] And when we grasp this point, we have come to the heart of the "iconic" nature of the model Lewis so admired. It is a difficult concept—time's imitation of eternity—but Lewis thought it was fundamental to the understanding of the medieval world.

For instance, in *Discarded Image*, Lewis provides a brilliant synthesis of some of the most severely dialectical arguments that make up *Consolation* V, the final chapter of Boethius's magnum opus, that part specifically concerned with the relationship between perpetuity and eternity. Although most of us think of "eternity" as that which goes "on and on," Boethius explains, we should actually call *that*, "perpetuity." Perpetuity is nothing more than an endless chain of brief moments, connected together. And given that eternity, on the other hand, is the "actual and timeless fruition of illimitable life," Boethius can call time an imitation of eternity. Time, as it were, is almost a "parody" of eternity, a "hopeless attempt to compensate for the transitoriness of its 'presents' by infinitely multiplying them."[23] God, of course, is not perpetual, but eternal. And so, what, in time, is spread out over an infinite number of moments, can be found gathered into a full and simultaneous perfection in God.

In other words, the world of time itself is a veil, behind which stands eternity, and Lewis was not reticent about his admiration of

---

[20]See Plato, *Timaeus* 27c.
[21]Calcidius, *On Plato's Timaeus*, 318.
[22]Calcidius, *On Plato's Timaeus*, 243.
[23]*DI*, 89.

this passage in Boethius. In fact, Lewis thought that Boethius had done a better job than Plato himself in explaining how the invisible and visible worlds are connected![24]

But this was not the first time Lewis attempted to expound the ancient idea of time imitating eternity. Decades earlier, in a long but important passage from his 1936 *Allegory of Love*, he used the synonymous terms *symbolism* and *sacramentalism* to get at this Platonic tradition transmitted to the medieval period by Calcidius and Macrobius. Appreciating the world's symbolism must begin, the scholar notes, with observing the crucial difference between "sacramentalism" and mere "allegory":

> If our passions, being immaterial, can be copied by material inventions [through allegory], then it is possible that our material world in its turn is the copy of an invisible world. As the god Amor and his figurative garden are to the actual passions of men, so perhaps we ourselves and our "real" world are to something else. The attempt to read that something else through its sensible imitations, to see the archetype in the copy, is what I mean by symbolism or sacramentalism. . . . To put the difference in another way, for the symbolist it is we who are the allegory. . . . The world which we mistake for reality is the flat outline of that which elsewhere veritably is in all the round of its unimaginable dimensions. . . .
>
> Symbolism comes to us from Greece. It makes its first effective appearance in European thought with the dialogues of Plato. The Sun is the copy of the Good. Time is a moving image of eternity. All visible things exist just in so far as they succeed in imitating the Forms. . . . [This is the] diffused Platonism, or Neoplatonism— if there is a difference—of Augustine, the pseudo-Dionysius, of Macrobius, of the divine popularizer Boethius.[25]

The whole world, then, can be read as a "symbol"—that is, a "copy," as in a mirror that distorts an image or a portrait that merely sums up a

---

[24]*DI*, 89-90.

[25]C. S. Lewis, *The Allegory of Love* (Oxford: Oxford University Press, 1958), 45-46.

likeness. When dealing with our earthly "images" or "copies" or "depictions," we know that the real thing is better: because it is alive, in motion, has color and depth. And so, we must apply this to the cosmos. It is copy. In a strange way, even the fundamental properties of physics (motion and space and time) are mere images, pointing to some more fundamental reality. This is what Chris Armstrong has called Lewis's "world-sacramentalism."[26]

SYMPHONY OF THE WORLD

But as I have already suggested, the major contention of this book is that we always have to keep in mind the "third Lewis," that is, the vernacularizer or popularizer who translated these abstract formulations of time's imitation of eternity into devotional and imaginative writings. And so, I would like to conclude this chapter with two quick examples to show how the new, British Boethius used his fiction to re-create (in a modern vernacular) what it felt like to "breathe" this medieval air.

In the creation scene found in *The Magician's Nephew*, Diggory and Jill, along with Uncle Andrew, the White Witch, and the cabby, are cast into Narnia before the world had been made. Standing there in the precosmic dark, when Narnia was yet formless and void, the ragtag group is able to watch as creation is sung into existence. At first, Diggory hears low notes "deep enough to be the voice of the earth herself."[27] It is "the most beautiful noise he had ever heard. It was so beautiful he could hardly bear it. The horse seemed to like it too; he gave a sort of whinny a horse would give if, after years of being a cab-horse, it found itself back in the old field where it had played as a foal."[28] But then something more wondrous takes place: that single melodic line becomes a rich tapestry of multiple melodies. It becomes a kind of medieval polyphony. The initial line is joined by "more voices than you could possibly count. They were in harmony with it, but far higher up the scale: cold, tingling,

---

[26]See his discussion of how medieval "sacramentality" can serve as a rejoinder to modern materialism in *Medieval Wisdom*, 147-64.

[27]C. S. Lewis, *The Magician's Nephew* (New York: HarperTrophy, 1984), 116.

[28]Lewis, *Magician's Nephew*, 116.

silvery voices."[29] These are the voices of the stars joining the symphony. Soon, "the Voice on the earth was now louder and more triumphant,"[30] as it sung the sun into being: "The eastern sky changed from white to pink and from pink to gold. The Voice rose and rose, till all the air was shaking with it. And just as it swelled to the mightiest and most glorious sound it had yet produced, the sun arose,"[31] and "you could imagine that it laughed for joy as it came up."[32] The song changes one more time: "The Lion was pacing to and fro about that empty land and singing his new song. It was softer and more lilting than the song by which he had called up the stars and the sun; a gentle, rippling music. And as he walked and sang the valley grew green with grass."[33] Polly notices that "when you listened to his song you heard the things he was making up: when you looked round you, you saw them. This was so exciting that she had no time to be afraid."[34] In this Mahler-like symphonic moment (I'm thinking especially of *Symphony* no. 1), Aslan has not only sung the earth, the stars, the sun, the flowers, and the animals into existence, but also let his song infuse his creatures, so that his song has become their song. The stars, the sun, the plants, the animals have their own personalities, but as lent to them by Aslan. The world is penetrated by song, and joy. It is a polyphonic world of beauty that leaves you "with open mouths and shining eyes."[35]

In a second passage, his brilliantly terrifying séance in "The Descent of the Gods," in *That Hideous Strength*, Ransom and Merlin are visited by the ancient planetary intelligences—that is, the pure, spiritual intellects of classical mythology descend, drawing all the affairs of the household into their spiritual fields. When the winged Mercury comes to visit, the household erupts in uproarious talk, outrageous banter, puns and jokes and arguments of ridiculous complexity: "Paradoxes, fancies,

---

[29]Lewis, *Magician's Nephew*, 116-17.
[30]Lewis, *Magician's Nephew*, 117.
[31]Lewis, *Magician's Nephew*, 119.
[32]Lewis, *Magician's Nephew*, 119.
[33]Lewis, *Magician's Nephew*, 123.
[34]Lewis, *Magician's Nephew*, 126-27.
[35]Lewis, *Magician's Nephew*, 118.

anecdotes, theories laughingly advanced yet (on consideration) well worth taking seriously, had flowed from them and over them with dazzling prodigality."[36] Next Venus comes, bringing with her sickeningly sweet tranquility and fragrances of "nard and cassia's balmy smells and all Arabia breathing from a box; even something more subtly sweet, perhaps maddening,"[37] while, upstairs, in Merlin "the inconsolable wound with which man is born waked and ached at this touching."[38] Mars comes, breathing into all a joyful, masculine, militant sense of confidence and camaraderie: "Their love for one another became intense. Each, looking on all the rest, thought: 'I'm lucky to be here. I could die with these."[39] Saturn brings feelings of infinite depth, and visions of height and profundity, and thoughts, tinged with cold melancholy, of eternity, of time, and profound depths,[40] before Jupiter arrives to cast a spell of big booming bells, ceremony, pomp, and festivity. Throughout this section, Lewis alternates his descriptions of the encounters with these "Oyarses" on the sensuous level of the flesh and emotions, as experienced in the kitchen below, with the higher perception into the eternal and spiritual realities, enjoyed by Ransom and Merlin in the room above.

But the important thing to note in these two passages, is that Lewis, "one of the finest Christian Platonists," as Louis Markos calls him,[41] set himself to re-create the medieval *harmonia mundi* of Macrobius, Boethius, and Calcidius, who had taught that the whole world is tuned "as with the seven tones of a plucked cithara."[42] For Calcidius (as well as for Cicero and Boethius) the heavens are quite literally a symphony: "The Pythagorean doctrine is that the world consists of harmonic ratio and that the celestial bodies, separated by intervals which are congruent and consonant with one another, produce musical sounds owing to the extremely rapid impulse of their flight. . . . Musical sounds are produced by stellar

---

[36]C. S. Lewis, *That Hideous Strength* (London: Scribner, 2003), 318.

[37]Lewis, *That Hideous Strength*, 319.

[38]Lewis, *That Hideous Strength*, 320.

[39]Lewis, *That Hideous Strength*, 321.

[40]Lewis, *That Hideous Strength*, 323.

[41]Markos, *From Plato to Christ: How Platonic Thought Shaped the Christian Faith* (Downers Grove, IL: InterVarsity Press, 2021), 202.

[42]Calcidius, *On Plato's Timaeus*, 239.

movement."[43] Lewis, having lectured on the passage for his students, was able to turn it into an imaginative world suitable for us moderns.

THE LOST CATHEDRAL

The long, Platonic tradition, then, taught Lewis two things: to see the world as a symphony but always to take this symphony (or cathedral) as a symbol or sacrament or transposition, which gestures at something beyond. The world itself is but a sketchy translation of a poem that no one has ever heard. And it is for this reason that Lewis's mind kept drifting back to cathedrals when he wanted to describe how the medieval cosmos "felt," because, like the medieval model, the cathedral rendered a dreamlike effect, in which viewers (both now and in the medieval period) are amazed by the myriad details; struck by how, at the same time, all of these details are framed out in a larger ordered and harmonious whole; and dazzled by how the surfaces seemed saturated in light. One medieval viewer (Jean de Jandun), an otherwise unknown professor at the University of Paris, wrote a short piece of "travel-writing" in 1323 (*Tractatus de laudibus Parisius*). In his short and overwrought rhetorical composition in praise of Paris and its buildings, Jean, arguably the original French narcissist, nevertheless gives us precious insight into what a medieval church "felt" like in contemporary eyes. He describes Notre Dame of Paris as "terrible" (by which he means awe-filled) and "multipartite" and "wondrous," and refers both to its splendor and its overlapping, interwoven patterns. He's "not so much overwhelmed by the fact that Notre-Dame is beautiful but that it is beautiful in so many ways. Some things are high, some low, some round, some square, smooth, ornate, intricate, colorful, gemlike, light-filled."[44]

But Jean also describes the cathedral as possessing "saturated" surfaces. For him, it is full to the point of excess. In another medieval writer, cited often by Lewis, Abbot Suger, who oversaw and wrote about the rebuilding of the first Gothic cathedral, we have a passage

---

[43]Calcidius, *On Plato's Timaeus*, 239.

[44]Jason M. Baxter, "What We Lost at Notre-Dame de Paris," *America*, April 13, 2020, www.americamagazine.org/sites/default/files/issue_pdf/ARI_04.13.20.pdf.

of similarly effusive praise. With delight, Abbot Suger comments on the "diversity of materials [such as] gold, gems, pearls," and on the mingling of "these different ornaments both new and old," and how his church has every precious stone mentioned in the book of Jeremiah (sardius, topaz, jasper, chrysolite, onyx, beryl, sapphire, emerald) except the carbuncle. In sum, this "multicolor" church "abound[s] most copiously" with colors. We might be struck by how "gaudy" and overdecorated this sounds, but Suger (and his contemporaries) loved how the senses were overloaded with an "excess" of meaning. When Suger entered into his cathedral, then, he felt like he was dwelling, as it were, "in some strange region of the universe which neither exists entirely in the slime of the earth nor entirely in the purity of Heaven; and that, by the grace of God, I can be transported from this inferior to that higher world in an anagogical manner."[45] Standing in a medieval cathedral gives you a kind of x-ray vision of the world. Meaning is everywhere, full and rich. The material world has been gathered to a saturation point. In a cathedral, then, the spiritual world feels like it is leaking in, and our response is to want to soar up and through and out. Simply look up any of the black-and-white photographs of Salisbury Cathedral, and you'll see what I mean.[46]

In short, such medieval and modern experiences of the cathedral help us reconstruct the sense of awe and fullness and saturation that Lewis himself felt when contemplating the medieval model. The very world in its ordinary operation in time and space presented an experience of "anagogy," an uplift of the heart, a sense of deep insight that comes to the threshold of worship. The world is too full, suffused by bright colors that cut and burn. Such medieval symbolism or (better) sacramentalism, as formulated in the Platonic tradition, is the key concept to hold in mind to appreciate what it felt like to "breathe" the atmosphere of the premodern world.

---

[45] *Abbot Suger on the Abbey Church of St. Denis and Its Art Treasure,* ed. and trans. Erwin Panofsky, 2nd ed. by Gerda Panofsky-Soergel (Princeton, NJ: Princeton University Press, 1979), 21.
[46] I'm thinking of the ones by the Edwardian architectural photography firm Bedford Lemere in particular.

CHAPTER TWO

BREATHING NARNIAN AIR

Lewis's Medieval Apprenticeship

> *It may be the beautiful, the terrible, the awe inspiring,*
> *the exhilarating, the pathetic, the comic, or the merely*
> *piquant. Literature gives the entrée to them all.*
>
> C. S. LEWIS, *AN EXPERIMENT IN CRITICISM*

BREATHING NARNIAN AIR

On more than one occasion, Lewis made passing comments about the magical properties of living in Narnia. When the Pevensie children had lived in Narnia long enough that, "if ever they remembered their life in this world it was only as one remembers a dream," they spoke in a new, high mode of discourse, in courtly cadences suited to their occupations (of pursuing the White Stag, courtship, lawmaking, and war) modeled on Thomas Malory: "Then said King Peter (for they talked in quite a different style now, having been Kings and Queens for so long), 'Fair Consorts, let us now alight from our horses and follow this beast into the thicket; for in all my days I never hunted a nobler quarry.'"[1] At another point, in *Prince Caspian*, we hear about

---

[1] C. S. Lewis, *The Lion, the Witch and the Wardrobe* (New York: HarperCollins, 1984), 184-85.

the salutary effects of breathing Narnian air. The narrator comments, "I don't think Edmund would have had a chance if he had fought Trumpkin twenty-four hours earlier. But the air of Narnia had been working upon him ever since they arrived on the island, and all his old battles came back to him, and his arms and fingers remembered their old skill. He was King Edmund once more."[2] Apparently, breathing Narnian air brings regal bearing, nobleness of heart, and maturity beyond years. Indeed, Lewis loved the metaphor, and thus, he frequently spoke of how such "atmosphere" or "climate" or "weather" or "landscape," or "microclimate," was the single most important thing in literature. We find him confessing in a March 1951 letter that he did not read novels "for the characters. It's more that for me a novel, or any work of art, is primarily a *Thing*, an Object, enjoyed for its color, proportions, atmosphere, its flavor—the Odyssey-ishness of the *Odyssey* or the Learishness of *K[ing] Lear*."[3] Similarly, if a boy reads Fennimore Cooper, he speculated, he was not necessarily after danger and excitement, but rather elementally pure "story," which he considered the most elusive and underappreciated aspect of literature: "Take away the feathers, the high cheek-bones, the whiskered trousers, substitute a pistol for a tomahawk, and what would be left? For I wanted not the momentary suspense but that whole world to which it belonged. . . . The one lay a hushing spell on the imagination; the other excites a rapid flutter of the nerves."[4] In contrast, he loathed *The Three Musketeers*, because it was nothing but a string of action moments: "[It] makes no appeal to me at all. The total lack of atmosphere repels me. There is no country in the book—save as a storehouse of inns and ambushes. There is no weather."[5]

Contemporary neuroscience has proven what Lewis knew in his bones: when reading fiction we do not use the same faculty we employ while, say, doing mathematics or reasoning through a philosophical

---

[2]C. S. Lewis, *Prince Caspian* (New York: HarperCollins, 1984), 106.
[3]*Letters*, 3:102.
[4]"On Stories," *EC*, 492.
[5]"On Stories," *EC*, 494.

proof. Reading fiction is more embodied, and literature creates worlds in which we are immersed, move around within, as if traveling through a variegated landscape, where we "hear" and "breathe in" ideas that, in other contexts, were merely academic opinions.[6] And so, although in his scholarly works (like *Discarded Image*) the professor of medieval literature does what we would expect (lays out facts about dates, books, and ideas of Plato, Calcidius, Macrobius, and Boethius), he was also always careful to supply his reader with concrete examples, so that they could also know how the idea *felt*. Indeed, this was Lewis's trademark as a scholar, teacher, and writer: his ability to *perform* ideas, to use his imaginative talent to create a *feeling* in which the ideas under consideration were no longer dead opinions sitting on the dissection table of the mind, like in Rembrandt's *Anatomy Lesson*, but rather made to live again. In this sense, he was a historian of psychology.[7] In a beautifully patient letter to a young admirer, Lewis once called this literary pursuit the quest for the "thing" in itself:

> Dear Joan—Thanks for your letter of the 3rd. You describe your Wonderful Night v. well. That is, you describe the place and the people and the night and the feeling of it all, very well—but not the thing itself—the setting but not the jewel. And no wonder! Wordsworth often does just the same. His Prelude (you're bound to read it about 10 years hence. Don't try it now, or you'll only

---

[6]See Annie Murphy Paul, "Your Brain on Fiction," *New York Times*, March 17, 2012, www .nytimes.com/2012/03/18/opinion/sunday/the-neuroscience-of-your-brain-on-fiction .html. In *Surprised by Joy*, Lewis continually uses landscapes to describe reading experiences, or reading experiences to get at landscapes. For instance, when living in Surrey, he learned not to compare landscapes but to love each in its particularity: "What delighted me in Surrey was its intricacy. My Irish walks commanded large horizons and the general lie of land and sea could be taken in at a glance. . . . But in Surrey the contours were so tortuous, the little valleys so narrow, there was so much timber, so many villages concealed in woods or hollows, so many field paths, sunk lanes, dingles, copses. . . . [To] walk in it daily gave one the same sort of pleasure that there is in the labyrinthine complexity of Malory or the *Faerie Queene*" (*SBJ*, 72).

[7]For an excellent assessment of Lewis's poetic "capacity to apprehend and re-enact a complex of thoughts, feelings, circumstances and characters in such a way that readers may re-live or experience (*nacherleben*) a world from which they would otherwise be quite cut off," see Dennis Danielson's "Intellectual Historian," in *Cambridge Companion to C. S. Lewis*, 43-57 (43).

spoil it for later reading) is full of moments in which everything except the thing itself is described. If you become a writer you'll be trying to describe the thing all your life: and lucky if, out of dozens of books, one or two sentences, just for a moment, come near to getting it across.[8]

In addition to "atmosphere" and "weather," Lewis also liked to call this elusive literary quality a text's "landscape." Some readers, he knew, "carry their resolute Englishry with them all over the Continent, mix only with other English tourists, enjoy all they see for its 'quaintness,' and have no wish to realize what those ways of life, those churches, those vineyards, mean to the natives"[9] and complain of "bad tea where [they] might have had excellent coffee," just as some nonscholarly readers "prefer not to be beyond the impression, however accidental, which an old work makes on a mind that brings to it a purely modern sensibility and modern conceptions."[10] "But," Lewis continues, "there is another sort of travelling and another sort of reading. You can eat the local food and drink the wines, you can share the foreign life, you can begin to see the foreign country as it looks, not to the tourist, but to its inhabitants. You can come modified, thinking and feeling as you did not think and feel before."[11] But this requires study. You "have to go outside [the poem]" so that you come back "inside it again, better equipped. (We have to go outside some medieval poems pretty often to look up hard words in a glossary or dictionary.)"[12] Given that the meanings of words shift over centuries, and sometimes shift so subtly that they can become hollowed out even without us detecting it, Lewis knew we have to try to encounter words "in [their] native habitat."[13] Old words have a "dangerous sense"—that is, "we are often deceived.

---

[8]*Letters*, 3:765.

[9]*DI*, x.

[10]C. S. Lewis, "De Audiendis Poetis," in *Studies in Medieval and Renaissance Literature*, Canto Classics (Cambridge: Cambridge University Press, 1998), 2.

[11]*DI*, 3.

[12]Lewis, "De Audiendis Poetis," 1.

[13]C. S. Lewis, *Studies in Words*, 2nd ed., Canto Classics (Cambridge: Cambridge University Press, 2013), 2.

In an old author, the word may mean something different. I call such senses dangerous senses because they lure us into misreadings."[14] Sometimes one comes to realize that "often after years of contented misreadings, one has been interpolating senses later than those the author intended."[15] But all such work "outside" the poem is always directed at getting back into the poem, getting back on the trail of that elusive so-called "kappa element," a term he coined by borrowing the first letter—*kappa*—from the Greek word *krypton* as a shorthand reference to the "hidden element" in a story. Indeed, as Michael Ward has argued, just as Lewis sought out literary "weather" as a reader, Lewis-the-writer borrowed from medieval myth and science to create a different planetary "atmosphere" for each of the books in his Narnian series: one breathes the atmosphere of Jupiter in *The Lion, the Witch and the Wardrobe*; Saturn provides the weather for *The Last Battle*; Venus the landscape for *The Magician's Nephew*; and so on. According to Ward, Lewis translated (or vernacularized) all of the medieval planetary system (as described in *Discarded Image*) into modern books for modern children.[16]

It would be missing the point to think of such a literary technique as a code to ensure some kind of secrecy. Rather, Lewis was "translating" ideas into literary worlds, which evoke different types of psychological responses. Readers of *Surprised by Joy* have long known the importance of Samuel Alexander's *Space, Time and Deity* for Lewis, a work he encountered in 1924 and provided him with a crucial terminological distinction: between "enjoyment" and "contemplation." Indeed, throughout his writing career, as the use of the metaphors of atmosphere, landscape, and weather attest, Lewis reflected on these different modes of engaging the world, and he practiced a kind of pivoting back and forth between one and the other. At times, he argues from facts about facts, but then he would step back inside of the

---

[14]Lewis, *Studies in Words*, 13.

[15]Lewis, *Studies in Words*, 1.

[16]For more on "atmosphere" and Alexander's importance for Lewis, see the subsection "Literary Reasons for Secrecy," in Michael Ward, *Planet Narnia: The Seven Heavens in the Imagination of C. S. Lewis* (Oxford: Oxford University Press, 2010), 15-19.

argument to look at it from what scholars of cinema call a "point of view shot." And although this sounds modern and edgy, here too, here again, we can hear echoes of old Boethius, who had made a similar distinction between perceiving the world according to ratio and seeing the world via the faculty of *intelligentia*.

For Boethius and the medieval intellectual tradition he inspired, there is a hierarchy of psychological powers of perception, each appropriate to a different rung of the ladder of creation. According to the fifth book of the *Consolation*,[17] the lowest level of taking in the world is sense perception, followed by the ability to picture things within (imagination), followed by reason (*ratio*), which is only surpassed by *intelligentia* or understanding. Each one of these powers of knowing is appropriate to different kinds of creatures: the clam, for example, has sense perception but no ability to picture things to itself like the dog or cat can do. Reason is the power of human beings, and *intelligentia* belongs properly only to God. And yet, Boethius hints that, in rare instances, God loans this way of seeing to human beings.[18] There are moments in which the human and divine horizons briefly intersect: "It is just possible even for us to climb up to the intelligential level and get a glimpse."[19] Thus, for Boethius, human beings spend most of their lives processing the world through *ratio*, the reason-using, argument-generating, fact-seeking rational faculty, but in exceptional moments the more elusive, intuitive, contemplative grasp—*intelligentia* or *intellectus*—opens up within and transcends *ratio*. In a difficult passage, Lewis explains this teaching in Boethius in terms that recall Alexander's distinction between "enjoyment" and "contemplation." Angels enjoyed a perfected form of *intelligentia*, which medieval philosophers thought of as the simple the simple and simultaneous grasp of the truth. In contrast, that so-very-human faculty of knowing, *ratio*, was the plodding, progressive approach toward truth, a movement which

---

[17]Explained at *DI*, 88, and following.
[18]Boethius, *Consolation of Philosophy* 5.5.11-12.
[19]*DI*, 89.

goes step-by-step, building proof on proof, amounting evidence. The medieval theologians liked to say that the difference between them was like the difference between rest and motion. On those occasions where we simply "see" a self-evident truth, we are using *intelligentia*, and enjoying a flash of *intellectus*. Human reasoning begins with such self-evident principles, builds on them, and tries to extend its knowledge. In short, our whole lives are passed in the struggle to connect "those frequent, but momentary, flashes of *intelligentia* which constitute *intellectus*."[20]

Although this passage is concerned with making razor-sharp academic distinctions, it's hard to overemphasize what a crucial set of ideas this was for Lewis, for his writing, and even for his life. We hear echoes of this alternation between *ratio* and *intelligentia* in his autobiographical description of that "Joy" he was haunted by. At moments, he tells us, he was made "sick with desire" with a "sickness better than health."[21] And to describe those haunting and transitory, split-second instances of inspiration, Lewis uses language similar to what we find in his description of Boethius: They were but "momentary flashes, seconds of gold scattered in months of dross, each instantly swallowed up"[22] (compare to his description of Boethius above: "Man's mental life is spent in laboriously connecting those frequent, but momentary, flashes of *intelligentia*"). And then in one of his most visually memorable essays, Lewis uses the quotidian experience of stepping into a dark garden shed as a way of thinking through these same psychological stances. At first, he looks at a beam of light suspended in the dusty air, but then positions his own eye to look "along" the beam:

> Instantly the whole previous picture vanished. I saw no toolshed, and (above all) no beam. Instead I saw, framed in the irregular cranny at the top of the door, green leaves moving on the

---

[20]*DI*, 157.

[21]*SBJ*, 119.

[22]*SBJ*, 119; cf. with the "frequent, but momentary, flashes of *intelligentia* which constitute *intellectus*" (*DI*, 157).

branches of a tree outside and beyond that 90 odd million miles
away, the sun. Looking along the beam, and looking at the beam
are very different experiences.[23]

This contrast between "looking along the beam" and "looking at the
beam"—that is, the distinction between leaning into a literary experience of *intelligentia* (as Boethius put it), or "breathing" it in, and ana-
lyzing structures (according to *ratio*)—not only pervades *Surprised by
Joy* but also defined his self-understanding of his scholarship.[24]

THE PURPOSE OF LITERATURE

Clearly then, this critical distinction between being "outside" a text
(the analysis of a text) or moving about within a literary landscape
from "inside" (enjoying it) was a cornerstone of Lewis's thought. The
scholar or serious student must engage in a certain amount of pedantic
activity in order to equip themselves with a "tolerable . . . outfit," that
is, have a preliminary sense for the idiosyncratic features they will
encounter in historically foreign landscapes, even if the ultimate goal
is always to leave the map behind: "To be always looking at the map
when there is a fine prospect before you shatters the 'wise passiveness'
in which landscapes ought to be enjoyed. But to consult the map
before we set out has no such ill effect. Indeed it will lead us to many
prospects; including some we might never have found by following our
noses."[25] But it is this weather or native habitat that makes the literature
of the past so precious, because it allows for an opportunity to recover
"what it all felt like from within" or "what the ritual meant to those who
enacted it." The literary scholar has access not just to ancient ideas but
also to ancient feelings, and thus has access to specimens even more
valuable than a paleontologist's prehistoric insect frozen intact within
amber. Fact-gathering anthropologists or word-collecting philologists
will always have to view the cultures they study from without, or look

---

[23]C. S. Lewis, "Meditation in a Toolshed," in *God in the Dock: Essays on Theology and Ethics*,
    ed. Walter Hooper (Grand Rapids, MI: Eerdmans, 1970), 212.
[24]For example, see *SBJ*, 165-69.
[25]*DI*, ix.

"at" the historical culture, but if literary scholars set themselves in the right position, they will look from within, or "breathe" it in:

> Anthropologists may describe to us what modern savages do; they may conjecture what our ancestors did. . . . We cannot get inside it; not directly. But if that experience had infused its quality into some other thing which we can get inside, then this other, more penetrable, thing would now be the only medium through which we can get back to the experience itself. Such a "more penetrable thing" might be provided by a work of plastic or literary art which we can still appreciate.[26]

As we can see, the real value of reading literature for Lewis is not extracting good moral lessons and correct opinions, but something more liberating, more capacious, more generous. Literature is the ability to fix "our inner eye,"[27] an act of looking. In the final, moving pages of *An Experiment in Criticism*, published near the end of his life in 1961, Lewis pours himself out in a desperate effort to sum up a lifetime of disparate and affectionate reading, and to save literature from the merely moral:

> What then is the good of—what is even the defense for—occupying our hearts with stories of what never happened and entering vicariously into feelings which we should try to avoid having in our own person? Or of fixing our inner eye earnestly on things that can never exist—on Dante's earthly paradise, Thetis rising from the sea to comfort Achilles, Chaucer's or Spenser's Lady Nature, or the Mariner's skeleton ship?[28]

---

[26]Lewis, "De Audiendis Poetis," 11. For this belief, too, Lewis was indebted to Owen Barfield, who believed that "philology helps one to understand the 'internal' feelings and sentiments of past epochs, rather than simply projecting one's contemporary consciousness upon them" (in Michael Vincent di Fuccia's formula, found in *Owen Barfield: Philosophy, Poetry, and Theology* [Eugene, OR: Veritas, 2016], 28n45). For an example of the sort of scholarship Lewis was distancing himself from, see John Fleming's description of the early twentieth-century English faculty's reduction of literary texts to philological mines in "Literary Critic," in *Cambridge Companion to Lewis*, 18-19.

[27]C. S. Lewis, *An Experiment in Criticism*, Canto Classics (Cambridge: Cambridge University Press, 1996), 137.

[28]Lewis, *Experiment*, 137.

Almost twenty years earlier, he had answered this by arguing that the well-read individual has a special share of prudence: a "man who has lived in many places is not likely to be deceived by the local errors of his native village: the scholar has lived in many times and is therefore in some degree immune from the great cataract of nonsense that pours from the press and the microphone of his own age."[29] But in *An Experiment in Criticism*, rather than describing it in negative terms (that is, arguing that learning makes us less likely to be deceived), he describes historical knowledge—especially as experienced through literature—in the positive terms of an "extension of our being":

> Those of us who have been true readers all our life seldom fully realise the enormous extension of our being which we owe to authors. We realise it best when we talk with an unliterary friend. He may be full of goodness and good sense but he inhabits a tiny world. In it, we should be suffocated. The man who is contented to be only himself, and therefore less a self, is in prison. My own eyes are not enough for me, I will see through those of others. Reality, even seen through the eyes of many, is not enough. I will see what others have invented. Even the eyes of all humanity are not enough. I regret that the brutes cannot write books. Very gladly would I learn what face things present to a mouse or a bee; more gladly still would I perceive the olfactory world charged with all the information and emotion it carries for a dog.[30]

Literature, then, creates worlds of imaginative atmosphere, with vision and weather and smell, an atmosphere we would suffocate without, and that enlarges our being when we read well. The reader, by breathing in, living in its habitat, fixing the eye of his or her heart, becomes "another self," is "aggrandized," "healed," "enlarged"—in short, the reader "transcends" the limitations of their merely historical and local condition, without annihilating their individuality: "But in reading great literature I become a thousand men yet remain

---

[29]*EC*, 580.
[30]Lewis, *Experiment*, 140.

myself. Like the night sky in the Greek poem, I see with a myriad eyes, but it is still I who see. Here, as in worship, in love, in moral action, and in knowing, I transcend myself; and am never more myself than when I do."[31]

This is the secret behind the efficacy of Narnian air. It is a belief he shared with Boethius, and the tenet that guided his nonscholarly writing—that is, Boethius helped him find his "vocational" calling to create literary worlds that did not beat audiences with Christian facts but, rather, rendered atmosphere in which Christianity could be seen according to *intelligentia*. In fact, he felt that by creating a "world" in which Christianity could be breathed, as opposed to being only thought about, he could help remove some of the associations of religion with hushed tones and medical sterilization that he, as a child, had found so off-putting:

> I thought I saw how stories of this kind [i.e., his Narnia stories] could steal past a certain inhibition which had paralysed much of my own religion in childhood. Why did one find it so hard to feel as one was told one ought to feel about God or about the sufferings of Christ? I thought the chief reason was that one was told one ought to. An obligation to feel can freeze feelings. . . . The whole subject was associated with lowered voices; almost as if it were something medical. But suppose that by casting all these things into an imaginary world, stripping them of their stained-glass and Sunday school associations, one could make them for the first time appear in their potency? Could one not thus steal past those watchful dragons? I thought one could.[32]

C. S. Lewis as Medieval Scribe

We have seen then that Boethius's distinction between *intelligentia* and *ratio*, like Alexander's distinction between enjoyment and contemplation, found its echo in Lewis's distinction between looking at and

---

[31]Lewis, *Experiment*, 141.
[32]"Sometimes Fairy Stories May Say Best What's to Be Said," *EC*, 528.

looking along the beam, and that this distinction helps us explain an important aspect of Lewis's self-perceived mission as a writer and scholar, as one who creates atmosphere in which old ideas and words become breathable, walkable, imaginary landscapes. But there was one more way in which medieval ideas about the craft of writing influenced Lewis's own thoughts on composition.

Much of medieval literature is what Lewis, in one scholarly article, refers to as "traditional poetry." Certain poems, such as the *Iliad* or the poems of Thomas Malory, are not individual acts of inspiration, but rather are more the works of a storyteller who, repeating the essential plot line, weaves new characters, themes, descriptions, or details into the basic outline he inherited, a kind of literary recycling. Lewis had analyzed, in particular, the Arthurian legends, which had been repeated, retold, translated, updated, and modified. Like a snowball rolling down a hill, they tended to become accumulations of the techniques and additions of all previous editions rather than a unique and unrepeatable literary vision. Lewis felt that critics in his age would dismiss an author as "derivative" and "unoriginal" who "merely" repeats what has been said before, or who does not invent his or her own personal style. But the greatest authors of the medieval period were just this: shapers, composers, and recyclers of old materials. Chaucer, Boccaccio, and Malory borrowed and translated, but also mended, updated, and altered. They wrote traditional poetry in the sense that they felt it their chief task to dress old stories in new garb. In other words, by adopting this medieval conception of the art of composition, Lewis could liberate himself from the need to be "original."

Within the medieval tradition, such literary recycling—what was called *imitatio*—was not distasteful. Rather, it was considered part of the "medieval apprenticeship tradition," whereby a *modernus* (a "modern" writer, as opposed to an ancient one) wrote a text within the authoritative framework provided by a model author.[33] In one

---

[33]In *The Conspiracy of Allusion: Description, Rewriting, and Authorship from Macrobius to Medieval Romance* (Leiden: Brill, 1999), Douglas Kelly has shown how the preface to Macrobius's *Saturnalia* in particular became an invaluable text for medieval literary theorists and practitioners, those writing in Latin and the vernacular alike. See also Douglas Kelly, ed., *The Medieval "Opus": Imitation, Rewriting, and Transmission in the French*

particularly influential passage from Macrobius's *Saturnalia*, the late antique author, much admired by Lewis, describes how he had compiled for his son a compendium of Latin and Greek classics.[34] Macrobius insists, nevertheless, that his *Saturnalia*—which copies huge passages from classical authors, word for word—does indeed constitute a unified body. It is not just a pile of ill-digested, anthologized passages; rather, the author has been, he says, like a bee who gathers sweet nectar from a variety of places, or like one who makes perfumes and takes "particular care that the specific odor of any ingredient not be perceptible, since they aim to blend all the aromatic essences into a single fragrant exhalation."[35] His own work of recycling and recombining thus became like a chorus whose many voices blend to become one. Macrobius then concludes, "You know how a chorus consists of many people's voices, and yet they all produce a single sound. . . . That is my goal for the present work: it comprises many different disciplines, many lessons, examples drawn from many periods, but brought together into a harmonious whole."[36] As Douglas Kelly has shown, this passage from Macrobius became a paradigm for later medieval authors. It became a model for a type of composition (an *imitatio*) that was marked by the clever incorporation and reappropriation of ancient authors.[37]

And so, medieval authors wrote in the same way they built: studding their own works with remains from the past, literary borrowings analogous to the ancient columns woven into the architectural fabric of Christian basilicas.[38] Nor did Lewis miss the analogy. In his essay "The

Tradition (Amsterdam: Rodopi, 1996); Jan Ziolkowski, "The Highest Form of Compliment: Imitatio in Medieval Latin Culture," in *Poetry and Philosophy in the Middle Ages: A Festschrift for Peter Dronke*, ed. John Marenbon (Leiden: Brill, 2001), 293-307.

[34]Macrobius, *Saturnalia*, preface, 1-2. For edition and translation, see *Saturnalia*, ed. and trans. Robert A. Kaster, Loeb Classical Library 510-12, 3 vols. (Cambridge, MA: Harvard University Press, 2011).

[35]Macrobius, *Saturnalia*, preface, 8.

[36]Macrobius, *Saturnalia*, preface, 9-10.

[37]Mark Kauntze, *Authority and Imitation: A Study of the Cosmographia of Bernard Silvestris* (Leiden: Brill, 2014), 132.

[38]For the medieval pleasure of finding the past renewed in the physical arts, see Beat Brenk, "*Spolia* from Constantine to Charlemagne: Aesthetics versus Ideology,"

'Morte d'Arthur,'" he argues that the modern reader need not be "surprised or dismayed" if what is the original and pure core of a medieval author evades us, because

> we are not reading the work of an independent artist; we are reading what is almost such a "traditional book." . . . Whatever he does Malory's personal contribution to the total effect cannot be very great, though it may be very good. We should approach the book not as we approach Liverpool Cathedral, but as we approach Wells Cathedral. At Liverpool we see what a particular artist invented. At Wells we see something on which many generations laboured, which no man foresaw or intended as it now is, and which occupies a position half-way between the works of art and those of nature.[39]

Once we are "clear that Laȝamon is not the author of the *Brut*, nor Johan of *Sawles Worde*, in the sense in which Jane Austen is the author of *Persuasion*," then we can come to appreciate the slow process of accretion and accumulation, the composition of the ages, "a process which is quite foreign to modern literature," which looks for "originality."[40] These traditional poets seem strange to us, because at once they "seem enslaved to their originals" but in another very "cavalier." They would never hesitate to "supplement them from their own knowledge and, still more, from their own imagination—touching them up, bringing them more fully to life."[41] In another passage worth quoting in full, Lewis likens the medieval compositional practice to painters who add new colors to an old panel:

> We might equally well call our medieval authors the most unoriginal or the most original of men. They are so unoriginal that they hardly ever attempt to write anything unless someone has

---

Dumbarton Oaks Papers 41 (1987): 103-9; Paul Binski, *Gothic Wonder: Art, Artifice, and the Decorated Style, 1290–1350* (New Haven, CT: Yale University Press, 2014).

[39]C. S. Lewis, "The 'Morte d'Arthur,'" in *Studies in Medieval and Renaissance Literature*, Canto Classics (Cambridge: Cambridge University Press, 1998), 110.

[40]C. S. Lewis, "The Genesis of a Medieval Book," in *Medieval and Renaissance Literature*, 36.

[41]Lewis, "Genesis of a Medieval Book," 36.

written it before. They are so rebelliously and insistently original that they can hardly reproduce a page of any older work without transforming it by their own intensely visual and emotional imagination, turning the abstract into the concrete, quickening the static into turbulent movement, flooding whatever was colorless with scarlet and gold.

They can no more leave their originals intact that we can leave our own earlier drafts intact when we fair-copy them. We always tinker and (as we hope) improve. But in the Middle Ages you did that as cheerfully to other people's work as to your own.[42]

Lewis's own thoughts on this medieval practice of imitative composition are of more than technical interest. Indeed, if we keep in mind his scholarly description of medieval writers tinkering and adding color, then we gain special insight into his craft as a writer. Take, for example, this description of Ransom's first impressions of the unfallen world of *Perelandra*. Dumbfounded by "the strange sense of excessive pleasure which seemed somehow to be communicated to him through all his senses at once,"[43] Ransom is shocked by life on this happy planet, sinless and saturated with joy. Perelandra is sensually overwhelming, without constituting any temptation of the flesh. In addition to such fragrances, it is characterized by a vivid, almost radioactive brilliance of color: "The water gleamed, the sky burned with gold. . . . The very names of green and gold, which he used perforce in describing the scene, was too harsh for the tenderness, the muted iridescence, of that warm evening, warm like summer noon, gentle and winning like early dawn."[44] Lewis tellingly adds, "The sky was pure, flat gold like the background of a medieval picture."[45] Lewis is adding color, but those

---

[42]Lewis, "Genesis of a Medieval Book," 38. Just after these words, he makes the allusion explicit: "If a great painter adds a few square feet (or even inches) of his own work to the canvas of a good, but less good, artist, he certainly modifies everything else that the picture contains; but then everything else modifies what he has added. His own work, if he is really a master, presupposes all the rest, is calculated to improve *this* picture. It would not improve any other. For the total result we cannot exclusively thank either painter."

[43]C. S. Lewis, *Perelandra: A Novel* (New York: Scribner, 2003), 33.

[44]Lewis, *Perelandra*, 32.

[45]Lewis, *Perelandra*, 32.

familiar with two important passages from Dante (*Purgatorio* 7 and *Purgatorio* 28), where the medieval Florentine master himself pulls out all the stops in order to describe a nature remade in the afterlife, will hear echoes everywhere in this passage from *Perelandra*. The so-called Valley of the Kings in *Purgatorio* 7, like Lewis's *Perelandra*, is dazzlingly bright and overwhelmingly fragrant, and here flowers and plants outshine the most brilliant gems and precious metals back on earth:

> Gold and fine silver, carmine and leaded white
> indigo, lignite bright and clear,
> an emerald after it has just been split,
>
> placed in that dell would see their brightness fade
> against the colors of the grass and flowers.[46]

Similarly, when the pilgrim returns to Eden in *Purgatorio* 28, the poet draws on each of the senses to make a poetically saturated scene. Dante's garden has "verdant foliage"; it is full of the soft light of early morning; the air is fragrant; there's a gentle breeze, dancing leaves, birds "practicing their craft," like medieval singers engaged in polyphony. There is also a stream that runs so pure that it makes "the purest here on earth" seem defiled.[47] The medieval poet's language is shifting and kaleidoscopic, just like Lewis's. We know in fact that Lewis had this particular canto of Dante in mind when he was composing *Perelandra*.[48] We also know that he adored medieval garden poetry. Commenting on the garden scene in *Roman de la Rose*, Lewis praises it as "Jean's highest reach as a poet. No one who remembers the fatuity of most poetical attempts to describe heaven—the dull catalogues of jewelry and mass-singing—will underrate this green park, with its unearthly peace, its endless sunshine and fresh grass and grazing flocks."[49] And so, when we compare Lewis's *Perelandra*

---

[46]Dante, *Purgatorio* 7.73-74, trans. Jean Hollander and Robert Hollander (New York: Random House, 2003).

[47]This list is drawn from Dante, *Purgatorio* 28.2, 3, 6, 7, 10, 15, 29-30, respectively.

[48]See Lewis's letter to Charles Brady, October 29, 1944, *Letters*, 2:629-30.

[49]C. S. Lewis, *The Allegory of Love* (Oxford: Oxford University Press, 1958), 153.

passage with its "gold" and iridescence and the very failure of the "names of green and gold" to his description of the medieval poet as painter, we see how deeply the medieval mode of *imitatio* affected Lewis's self-understanding of his craft. Just as Malory rewrote the legends of Arthur that he inherited, just as Chaucer translated and touched up his borrowings from Boccaccio, and just as Dante "translated" the cosmology of his age into verse—when Lewis sat down to write, he participated in a similar authorial process, a paradoxical "slavish" imitation combined with the most "cavalier" creativity. He composed in the same way as those medieval authors he studied as a scholar. Lewis borrows them, intensifies them, adds color. *Perelandra* turns out to be Dante and Jean de Meun in space.

Conclusion: Grasping with the Heart

Throughout this chapter, I've argued that Lewis not only borrowed old *ideas* but even learned his craft of composition from the authors he studied. The important thing was not necessarily inventing or concocting in an original style, but to renew, recycle, enliven the original, so that the old vision would be credible to those who live in an incredulous age. The artist's duty (just like the scholar's) is to render atmosphere, so that one can breathe the air of the original. But Lewis did the same thing in his devotional works. And so, given that I've already provided several examples of fictional rehabilitations, I'd like to conclude this chapter by describing one last borrowing in the context of Lewis's writing on private prayer.

In his epistolary exchange with "Malcolm," Lewis at one point describes a process of prayer that he calls "festooning," according to which he borrowed a certain biblical passage, paused over it, thought on it, and then rephrased it, laying on new and fresh thoughts (hence "festooning") so that the scriptural passage would take on freshness without losing the plain sense. For instance, when praying "Thy kingdom come," Lewis mentally adds, "That is, may your reign be realized here, as it is realized there. But I tend to take *there* . . . as in the sinless world beyond the horrors of animal and human life; in the

behavior of stars and trees and water, in sunrise and wind. May there
be *here* (in my heart) the beginning of a like beauty."[50] Lewis then
comments on how he transforms "Thy will *be done*": "A great deal of
it is to be done by God's creatures, including me. The petition, then, is
not merely that I may patiently suffer God's will but also that I may
vigorously do it. I must be an agent as well as a patient."[51] These passages give us an enticing window into the quiet devotion of a great
man, and, clearly, they were meant to intrigue "Malcolm" who wrote
to ask his friend for more words on the subject.[52]

Here, as Armstrong has perceptively noted, we have a modern-
ization of the widespread medieval practice of *lectio divina*, a slow,
monastic, prayerful, meditative "holy reading" in which boundaries
between commentary and prayer are porous. In the words of Duncan
Robertson, medieval *lectio divina* was a fluid "movement of reading
into prayer."[53] One medieval "best seller," written by a Carthusian,
Hugh of Balma, describes how to pray through the "Our Father," phrase
by phrase, and sometimes word by word, lingering over each bit, ques-
tioning each phrase, and trying to get it to release its inner fragrance.
When we read, "Our Father, who art in heaven," we immediately pause,
says Hugh, and consider how we are privileged to call God "*our*" father.
God is not the special property of a religious elite, a Being known only
to a lofty priesthood, but he draws "all rational spirits" to himself. Next,
we come to "who art *in heaven*." Hugh meditates on the nature of the
heavens, and he wonders at how the nighttime sky is both beautiful,
steadfast, and continuously in motion. Thinking about *that*, Hugh,
briefly drawing on the language of desire from Song of Songs, dwells

---

[50]C. S. Lewis, *Letters to Malcolm: Chiefly on Prayer* (New York: Harvest Books, 1964), 25.

[51]Lewis, *Letters to Malcolm*, 26.

[52]See Lewis, *Letters to Malcolm*, 24.

[53]See Armstrong's "Getting Passionate," in *Medieval Wisdom*, 165-90. For the general back-
ground, see Duncan Robertson, *Lectio Divina: The Medieval Experience of Reading*, Cis-
tercian Studies 238 (Collegeville, MN: Liturgical Press, 2011), 134. See also the classic by
Jean Leclercq, *The Love of Learning and the Desire for God: A Study of Monastic Culture*
(New York: Fordham University Press, 1982). Interested readers can also consult my
Introduction to Christian Mysticism: Recovering the Wilderness of the Spiritual Life (Grand
Rapids, MI: Baker Academic, 2021).

on what it would be like to have this star-like constancy, this inner steadfastness. Hugh goes on like this for another thirty pages.[54]

The same type of slow, prayerful meditation on the Our Father can be found in Francis of Assisi, Angela of Foligno, and, perhaps most importantly for Lewis, in Dante. On the terrace of the prideful in the *Purgatorio*, the penitent sinners circle around the mountain, reciting the Lord's Prayer, but now the old, familiar prayer has been transformed. Indeed, Dante's audience would have been surprised to hear the long-familiar text, not in Latin, but in the "homely" language of everyday speech. And when we look closer, we realize that Dante has not simply translated the prayer word for word into Italian; rather, his souls perform a kind of spontaneous rewriting of the biblical and liturgical prayer, in which the forty-nine words of the Latin prayer become an Italian prayer of more than 160. Apparently, Dante was doing his own festooning:

> O our Father, you who reside in the heavens,
> not as one limited, but because of the greater love
> you have for those first effects there on high:
>
> praised be your name and your power
> by every creature, given that it is fitting
> to render thanks for your sweet breath.
>
> May the peace of your kingdom come to us,
> for if it doesn't come toward us, we are impotent by ourselves,
> even if we try with all of the strength of our intellect.
>
> And just as angels render their own desires
> Up to you as sacrifice, singing 'Hosanna,'
> So too may human beings do the same with theirs.
>
> Give to us today the daily manna
> without which he who grows weary in going forward
> goes backward through this dry desert.

---

[54]*Carthusian Spirituality: The Writings of Hugh of Balma and Guigo de Ponte*, trans. Dennis Martin, Classics of Western Spirituality (Mahwah, NJ: Paulist Press, 1997), 89-90.

And as we take that evil we have suffered
And pardon it, to every man: you, too, pardon,
With clemency, and you do not consider whether we have merit.

This, our virtue that is overcome so easily,
don't put it to the test by the ancient adversary,
but deliver us from him who goads it [to evil].

This last prayer, dear Lord,
is now not offered for ourselves, for whom there is no need,
but for those who remain behind us.[55]

This is the prayer recited by the souls who are trying to work off their prideful tendencies. We hear snatches of the scriptural original, but they are continually transformed, expanded, or slightly altered, so as to take on new meanings. The prayer is a kind of spontaneous act of performed meditation, and it constitutes one example among many of medieval, prayerful reading of Scripture. In other words, what "Malcolm" found so innovative (Lewis's "festooning") was a resuscitation of a common medieval meditative practice. This is what I mean by Lewis having learned his craft of writing from the medieval authors he studied.

---

[55]Dante, *Purgatorio* 11.1-24, translation mine.

CHAPTER THREE

From SYMPHONY *to* MACHINE

The Death of Antiquity and the Birth of the World of Speed

We do not look at trees either as Dryads or as beautiful objects while we cut them into beams: the first man who did so may have felt the price keenly, and the bleeding trees in Virgil and Spenser may be far-off echoes of that primeval sense of impiety. The stars lost their divinity as astronomy developed, and the Dying God has no place in chemical agriculture.

C. S. LEWIS, *ABOLITION OF MAN*

STRANGE AS IT MAY SOUND, Lewis hated cars. And newspapers. What are for most of us the banal and indispensable necessities of daily life were for Lewis sacraments of modernity. In a remarkable passage in *Surprised by Joy*, Lewis describes the blessing of not growing up in the world of automobiles:

> The deadly power of rushing about wherever I pleased had not been given me. I measured distances by the standard of man, man walking on his two feet, not by the standard of the internal

combustion engine. I had not been allowed to deflower the very idea of distance; in return I possessed "infinite riches" in what would have been to motorists "a little room." The truest and most horrible claim made for modern transport is that it "*annihilates space*." It does. It annihilates one of the most glorious gifts we have been given. It is a vile inflation which lowers the value of distance, so that a modern boy travels a hundred miles with less sense of liberation and pilgrimage and adventure than his grandfather got from traveling ten.[1]

In a second passage in *Surprised by Joy* Lewis targets newspaper reading, mocking the falsity of the desire to be up to date, which he labeled an "appalling waste of time and spirit." Those who do read the newspaper acquire "an incurable taste for vulgarity and sensationalism and the fatal habit of fluttering from paragraph to paragraph to learn how an actress has been divorced in California, a train derailed in France, and quadruplets born in New Zealand."[2] With age, Lewis grew more and more pessimistic about modernity, how it tends to "annihilate space" and increase in speed,[3] melt down everything into "liquid modernity" (to borrow a phrase from Zygmunt Bauman), and to occupy our minds with an endless and meaningless rush of flotsam and jetsam. The bustle and self-importance of these "real-world" concerns permeate our minds, and make us feel that the task of study and attentiveness are somehow unimportant, outdated, or passé.

In high contrast to this disdain for machines and the anxiety-inducing desire to be in the know and up to date, we have a youthful poem written by Lewis in 1919, full of reverent sentiment for old Oxford, which he praised for its cool freshness and its air of ancient solemnity. Oxford was a haven (or, perhaps, a preserve) for "useless" studies, a slow and dreamy city by design, and one of the last in the world where ancient streams and premodern poetry still made sense (a kind of academic Rivendell):

---

[1] *SBJ*, 157.
[2] *SBJ*, 159.
[3] *SBJ*, 157.

It is well that there are palaces of peace
And discipline and dreaming and desire,
Lest we forget our heritage and cease
The Spirit's work—to hunger and aspire . . .

But this shall never be: to us remains
One city that has nothing of the beast,
That was not built for gross, material gains,
Sharp, wolfish power or empire's glutted feast.

We are not wholly brute. To us remains
A clean, sweet city lulled by ancient streams,
A place of visions and of loosening chains,
A refuge of the elect, a tower of dreams.

She was not builded out of common stone
But out of all men's yearning and all prayer
That she might live, eternally our own,
The Spirit's stronghold—barred against despair.[4]

Later, when Lewis felt that Oxford had been overrun by the forces of industrialism, he announced his new preference for what was still the "country town" of Cambridge, where he was "most gratefully and happily, domiciled in a small college."[5] It reminded him of what Oxford had been in his younger and more vulnerable days: "The relief, the liberation, strike me afresh almost every day. In a way it is an eerie relief, for I seem to have recovered the past."[6] The depth of his feelings on this subject can also be found in a passage from *That Hideous Strength,* where he imagines his "clean, sweet city lulled by ancient streams" violently rent by mechanized modernity. In a fateful college meeting, the fellows of Bracton College decide to sell the ancient Bragdon Wood to a modern, industrial research center. The few traditional opponents are pilloried as "die-hards" and are made to seem

---

[4]Published as "Oxford," under the pseudonym Clive Hamilton, in *Spirits in Bondage* (London: Heinemann, 1919), 82-83.
[5]"Interim Report," *EC,* 638-43 (639).
[6]"Interim Report," *EC,* 638.

absurd, caricatured as curmudgeonly reactionaries who "passionately desired to see Bragdon surrounded with barbed wire."[7] And when a venerable, older don rises to his feet to propose a counterargument, he is shamed into silence: "Jewel had been already an old man in the days before the first war when old men were treated with kindness, and he had never succeeded in getting used to the modern world."[8] The world is now moving so fast that to not move is reactionary. But then in a passage that must have physically pained Lewis to write, he describes the fateful moment in which the old world of peaceful streams is wrenched apart by the new world of machines. Laborers move their heavy machinery into the college to tear up the garden. One evening in particular, the fellows hear "such noises as had never been heard in that room before—shouts and curses and the sound of lorries heavily drumming past or harshly changing gear, rattling of chains, drumming of mechanical drills, clanging of iron, whistles, thuddings, and an all pervasive vibration."[9] From within the college, the fellows can hear and feel the forces of speed and machinery undertake "the conversion of an ancient woodland into an inferno of mud and noise and steel and concrete."[10]

Perhaps Lewis was aware of how almost laughably grumpy it was to condemn what are, for us, innocuous modern conveniences, in a similar way to how all the children burst out laughing at Professor Kirk at the end of The Last Battle: "'Bless me, what do they teach them at these schools!' The older ones laughed. It was so exactly like the sort of thing they had heard him say long ago in that other world."[11] And yet, as we can see, behind those irascible, curmudgeonly lamentations about newspapers and cars stands a well-thought-out conviction that the whole world picture had changed, from the slow, contemplative, symphonic world (discussed in chap. 1) to the world of speed, bustle, and machine. More importantly, such changes in our

---

[7]C. S. Lewis, That Hideous Strength (London: Scribner, 2003), 26.

[8]Lewis, That Hideous Strength, 26.

[9]Lewis, That Hideous Strength, 88.

[10]Lewis, That Hideous Strength, 88.

[11]C. S. Lewis, The Last Battle (New York: HarperCollins, 1984), 194-95.

background picture or model—our "cosmic imaginary"—had a cascade of consequences. As we will see in this chapter and the next, how we think the world works—especially as related to whether we think time and space are "imitations of eternity," transpositions of supersensible realities—affects what we think a human being is (our psychology). Our psychology, in turn, influences our ethics and pedagogy, but also our understanding of language, and that in turn affects our sense of what makes for good style! And so understanding the rise of modernity was critical for the New Boethius's diagnosis and treatment of the maladies of the new barbarians. In the remainder of this chapter, I will sketch out the historical changes in world picture, and thus the social and psychological consequences that accompanied the shift from perceiving the world as a symphony to perceiving it as a machine.

From Contemplation to Control

As is evident from Lewis's denigration of cars and mockery of newspapers, the Oxford professor thought that one of the most defining characteristics that separate us—the denizens of late modernity—from *any* other historical period is summed up by a phrase used by historians of science, the "mechanization of the world picture"—that is, the increasing tendency to see the world as if it were a machine. The story of modernity is, as everyone knows, intimately bound up with the rise of empirical science during the scientific revolution, and the scientific revolution was itself tied up with new instruments that were used to measure, quantify, and magnify: modern cartography, the clock, the barometer, the telescope, the microscope, linear perspective, and eventually technologies such as the steam engine, the telegram, and industrial machinery. In a story that has often been rehearsed, the hylozoistic universe (or soul-infused universe, almost as if the world were a living organism) of desire and intelligence and sympathies yielded to the inanimate world of mechanistic structures and mathematized qualities. For Plato and Aristotle and Calcidius down to Dante, the heavens were crystalline spheres, and the motion of the luminous bodies were the visible manifestation of operations of intelligences whose gaze was locked on eternity. This ancient and medieval fabric of the heavens began to unravel, though, when Galileo revealed "flaws" in the heavens. With his intrepid telescope, he pried into the "perfect region" of the heavens, finding eighty stars within Orion's belt, which had been too faint to see with the unaided eye. Galileo also found not only that there were spots on the sun but also that they moved across its surface. All of this strengthened his then-controversial conviction that, as Steven Shapin puts it, "studying the properties of ordinary earthly bodies could afford understanding of what nature was like universally."[12] Such a statement has become so obvious that it is difficult to feel its historical import, but for someone like Calcidius, who was moved to worshipful rapture through the contemplation of the artistry of the heavenly realm, the discovery of moons orbiting Jupiter would have meant that our moon, which had been thought unique, the mysterious cause of earthly "lunacy," the boundary marker of the realm of air and ether, was downgraded to just one among many stones darting in and out of the shadow of a larger body. And, crushingly, Newton's proof that the elliptical orbits of planets were due to universal gravitation meant, too, that planets fall through space in just the same way a terrestrial projectile, say balls of various size dropped from a tower, fall toward the earth. All this meant that the operation of the heavens could no longer be considered as designed in order to display a delicate harmonic pattern: apparently their paths were not laid out to figure forth Platonic solids (as Kepler had rhapsodically suggested), and their motion was not the propulsion due to an outpouring of love from intelligent beings. Space was made up of a bunch of rocks orbiting about chemical reactions. Newton also declared what previous centuries had been hesitantly hinting at: There are no crystalline spheres; luminous bodies are not suspended in ether; stars are not like gems in a band but, rather, are spread out throughout an infinite void. In this way, the inward-looking

---

[12]Steven Shapin, *The Scientific Revolution*, 2nd ed. (Chicago: University of Chicago Press, 2018), 18.

cosmos, the cosmos of "transposition," which had existed *in order to* translate into the harmonic ordering of time and space the deep perception of eternity, lost its metaphorical value. That is, its order could not be read as specifically designed to reveal, *iconically*, the eternal paradigm. A contemporary of Lewis's, Alexandre Koyre, summed up the changes this way:

> This scientific and philosophical revolution . . . can be described roughly as bringing forth the destruction of the Cosmos, that is, the disappearance, from philosophically and scientifically valid concepts, of the conception of the world as a finite, closed, and hierarchically ordered whole . . . and its replacement by an indefinite and even infinite universe which is bound together by its fundamental components and laws, in which all these components are placed on the same level of being. This, in turn, implies the discarding of scientific thought of all considerations based upon value-concepts, such as perfection, harmony, meaning and aim, and finally the utter devalorization of being, the divorce of the world of value and the world of facts.[13]

And to put it in contemporary terms, we can cite physicist Steven Weinberg: "The more the universe seems comprehensible, the more pointless it also seems."[14] For seventeenth-century people, this was even more difficult to accept. John Donne famously lamented that the "circles" had been broken, by which he meant that the medieval model, in all of its interlocking harmonic perfection, was falling apart:

> And new philosophy calls all in doubt,
> The element of fire is quite put out,
> The sun is lost, and th'earth, and no man's wit
> Can well direct him where to look for it.

---

[13]Alexandre Koyre, *From the Closed World to the Infinite Universe* (Baltimore: Johns Hopkins University Press, 1968), 2.

[14]Quoted by Michael Ruse, "Atheism, Naturalism and Science: Three in One?," in *The Cambridge Companion to Science and Religion*, ed. Peter Harrison (Cambridge: Cambridge University Press, 2010), 221.

And freely men confess that this world's spent,
When in the planets and the firmament
They seek so many new; they see that this
Is crumbled out again to his atomies.
'Tis all in pieces, all coherence gone,
All just supply, and all relation.[15]

The last lines of Donne's poem are especially telling: "'Tis all in pieces . . . / All just supply, and all relation." They refer not only to the loss of a sense of the heavenly intelligences (the "hylozoistic" component) but also to its replacement by the mechanization of the world picture—that is, in place of "substantial forms," ghostly essences that imbue matter with real qualities, Galileo, Descartes, and Boyle made a distinction between "primary qualities" and "secondary qualities." Primary qualities were those properties that could be described as extensions in space (size, shape, arrangement, and motions). Secondary qualities were the ways in which these various primary qualities affected what is produced *subjectively* in us. As Shapin summarizes it, "Only *some* of our ideas of bodies might now be treated as objective. . . . Other experiences and ideas would have now to be regarded as subjective—the result of how our sensory apparatus actively processes impressions deriving from the real, primary realm." In this way, "micromechanical reality took precedence over common experience, and subjective experience was severed from accounts of what objectively existed."[16] And so we live in a world that is in actuality flavorless, odorless, and colorless, a series of interlocking microstructures whose various mathematical extensions and motions create within the human mind different subjective impressions.

As the sixteenth century was his particular period of specialization, Lewis was intimately aware of the details and cultural consequences of the changing world picture. Indeed, he characterized the scientific revolution as a period of new learning and new ignorance. ("New

---

[15]John Donne, "The Anatomy of the World," www.poetryfoundation.org/poems/44092/an-anatomy-of-the-world.
[16]Shapin, *Scientific Revolution*, 53.

Learning and New Ignorance" is the title of the introductory chapter in his *English Literature in the Sixteenth Century*.) Lewis irreverently calls the hallowed scientific revolution a period of "new ignorance" because he believed that by choosing to focus on quantifiable measurements to the exclusion of all other types of inquiry, modern science had brought modern culture into an ethical and social desert, on account of its willful suspension of "judgements of value" and its decision to strip nature of all "qualitative properties" and to "ignore its final cause (if any), and treat it in terms of quantity."[17] In other words, when the cosmos is not perceived as "iconic," having a meaning and a purpose, it turns into a lump of inert matter passively awaiting us to "dominate and use it for our own convenience."[18] In fact, Lewis points out that science and magic are more closely related than modern science would like to admit, because in essence they have pursued their crafts with the same end in mind. The modern world took up "the magician's bargain: give up our soul, get power in return."[19] The only reason it preferred science to magic is because science worked:

> If we compare the chief trumpeter of the new era (Bacon) with Marlowe's Faustus, the similarity is striking. You will read in some critics that Faustus has a thirst for knowledge. In reality, he hardly mentions it. It is not truth he wants from the devils, but gold and guns and girls. . . . The true object is to extend Man's power to the performance of all things possible. He rejects magic because it does not work; but his goal is that of the magician. . . . It might be going too far to say that the modern scientific movement was tainted from its birth: but I think it would be true to say that it was born in an unhealthy neighbourhood and at an inauspicious hour. Its triumphs may have been too rapid and purchased at too high a price: reconsideration, and something like repentance, may be required.[20]

---

[17]C. S. Lewis, *The Abolition of Man* (New York: Touchstone, 1996), 69.
[18]Lewis, *Abolition of Man*, 69.
[19]Lewis, *Abolition of Man*, 72.
[20]Lewis, *Abolition of Man*, 78.

All of this—the movement from an iconic cosmos to a mechanized one—is what Charles Taylor hauntingly called "excarnation." In a past "enchanted age" there was a "strong sense" of the sacred, which "marks out certain people, times, place, and actions" and is "by its very nature localizable, and its place is clearly marked out in ritual and sacred geography."[21] Our modern world, on the other hand, is haunted by a sense of loss: "This is what we sense, and often regret the passing of, when we contemplate the medieval cathedral. God-forsakenness is an experience of those whose ancestral culture has been transformed and repressed by a relentless process of disenchantment, whose deprivations can still be keenly felt."[22] The result is that the sacred is felt to have withdrawn from the physical, visible world, or, in the words of Ransom to Merlin, "Whatever of spirit may still linger in the earth has withdrawn fifteen hundred years further away from us since your time."[23]

Lewis himself referred to this historical shift—what Taylor calls "excarnation"—as "the process that has led us from the living universe where man meets the gods to the final void where almost-nobody discovers his mistakes about almost-nothing."[24] In his Cambridge inaugural address ("De Descriptione Temporum"), the magisterial third book in *Abolition of Man*, his chapter "New Learning and New Ignorance," and several occasional talks, essays, and reviews (such as "The Empty Universe"), Lewis described such a process as the slow spread of a spiritual cancer, which began by disenchanting the universe, moved to demystifying the human body, and ended by casting doubt on the very possibility of rationality:

> At the outset the universe appears packed with will, intelligence, life and positive qualities; every tree is a nymph and every planet a god. Man himself is akin to the universe. The advance of knowledge gradually empties this rich and genial universe: first

---

[21]Charles Taylor, *A Secular Age* (Cambridge, MA: Belknap, 2007), 553.

[22]Taylor, *Secular Age*, 553.

[23]Lewis, *That Hideous Strength*, 285-86.

[24]C. S. Lewis, "The Empty Universe," in *Present Concerns*, ed. Walter Hooper (London: Harcourt Brace Jovanovich, 1986), 81.

of its gods, then of its colors, smells, sounds and tastes, finally solidity itself. . . . As these items are taken from the world, they are transferred to the subjective side of the account: classified as our sensations, thoughts, images or emotions. The Subject be-comes gorged, inflated, at the expense of the Object. But the matter does not rest there. The same method which has emptied the world now proceeds to empty ourselves.[25]

Accompanying the evaporation of soul from the world come changes in the linguistic landscape. We move from a language of metaphors "with phantom longings and endeavors" to a "universe with phantom police-courts and traffic regulations," or, in other words, a world of desire and intelligence to a world of mechanical "laws."[26] The results of the mechanization of the world picture is that spiritual longing has come to feel out of place. And, as we will see in a later chapter, this longing is a theme that haunted the medieval scholar's essays, fiction, and even his autobiography.

In sum, while the medieval cosmos was alive, a great living being, a world that moved because it experienced desire, for modernity the world is made up of passive lumps of matter, waiting to be acted on by forces, suspended within space. (The word *space* in this sense is a modern coinage.) It is a place "of cold, eternal silences": "The funda-mental concept of modern science is, or was till very recently, that of natural 'laws.' . . . In medieval science the fundamental concept was that of certain sympathies, antipathies, and strivings inherent in matter itself."[27] In modernity, human beings prefer to describe rocks as falling in obedience to a law, whereas medieval people spoke of the rock as desiring, longing to return to its natural place, like a pigeon flying back to its nest by a homing instinct. In this way, the medieval cosmos, satu-rated with presence and soul, was densely alive and exerted a moral pull on the soul and mind. It was an "orchestra," "tingling with

---

[25]Lewis, "The Empty Universe," 81.
[26]C. S. Lewis, "Imagination and Thought in the Middle Ages," in *Studies in Medieval and Renaissance Literature*, Canto Classics (Cambridge: Cambridge University Press, 1998), 50.
[27]*DI*, 92.

anthropomorphic life, dancing, ceremonial, a festival not a machine. It is very important to grasp this at the outset. If we do not, we shall constantly misread our poets by taking for highly conceited metaphor expressions which are still hardly metaphorical at all."[28] But even more fascinating is the social changes that came about as a result of changes in cosmic imaginaries.

THE GREAT DIVIDE

All of this was of more than academic interest for Lewis, because he perceived that, over time, changes in cosmology were accompanied by corresponding changes in psychology and ethics. According to the model, there was a threefold, cosmological hierarchy: "Stellar powers command, the angelic beings execute, and the terrestrials obey," a tripartite arrangement in terms reflected in the powers of the human soul. The "rational part lives in the body's citadel (*capitolium*), that is, the head. In the camp or barracks (*castra*) of the chest, warrior-like, the 'energy which resembles anger,' that which make a man high-spirited, has its station. Appetite, which corresponds to the common people, is located in the abdomen below them both."[29] But if the cosmos had been, so to speak, morally gutted, with its moral desire removed, become all matter and forces, then, analogously, "the individual is to become all head. The human race is to become all Technocracy."[30] In Lewis's analysis, in both modern cosmology and in modern psychology, that third part of the triad (the spirit) had gone missing, and so reason becomes a mere calculating machine. Lewis called this the "narrowing" of the meaning of reason: "From meaning . . . the whole Rational Soul, both *intellectus* and *ratio*, it shrank to meaning merely 'the power by which man deduces one proposition from another.'"[31]

But the final step in Lewis's sketch of the cultural consequences of the scientific revolution was to trace out the political and

---

[28]C. S. Lewis, *English Literature in the Sixteenth Century* (Oxford: Oxford University Press, 1954), 4.

[29]*DI*, 57.

[30]Lewis, *That Hideous Strength*, 256.

[31]*DI*, 158-59.

sociological effects. If human beings are just calculating machines, and human society is a vast network of processors, then political leaders are like the operators of a large piece of machinery, sending information and commands through the circuitry. Indeed, Lewis thought not only that "between [Sir Walter] Scott's age and ours" there was a profound change in the ideal of political order, but also that these changes had collapsed the distinctions between "democracies" and "dictatorships":

> If I wished to satirise the present political order I should borrow for it the name which *Punch* invented during the first German War: *Govertisement*. This is a portmanteau word and means "government by advertisement." But my intention is not satiric; I am trying to be objective. The change is this. In all previous ages that I can think of the principal aim of rulers, except at rare and short intervals, was to keep their subjects quiet, to forestall or extinguish widespread excitement and persuade people to attend quietly to their several occupations. And on the whole their subjects agreed with them. They even prayed (in words that sound curiously old-fashioned) to be able to live "a peaceable life in all godliness and honesty" and "pass their time in rest and quietness." But now the organisation of mass excitement seems to be almost the normal organ of political power. We live in an age of "appeal," "drives," and "campaigns." Our rulers have become like schoolmasters and are always demanding "keenness." And you notice that I am guilty of a slight archaism in calling them "rulers." "Leaders" is the modern word. I have suggested elsewhere that this is a deeply significant change of vocabulary. Our demand upon them has changed no less than theirs on us. For of a ruler one asks justice, incorruption, diligence, perhaps clemency; of a leader, dash, initiative, and (I suppose) what people call "magnetism" or "personality."[32]

---

[32] C. S. Lewis, "De Descriptione Temporum," in *Selected Literary Essays*, ed. Walter Hooper, Canto Classics (Cambridge: Cambridge University Press, 1969), 8.

For all of these reasons, Lewis could assert, in his Cambridge address, that "the greatest of all divisions in the history of the West" is "that which divides the present from, say, the age of Jane Austen and Scott."[33] More important than the gap between, say, Egypt and Greece, or ancient Rome and the Christian era, or between the medieval period and the early modern period, was the transformative period that he himself had been born at the very end of. The great paradigm shift, according to which changes in cosmology trickled down over the course of centuries to slowly make up new psychological and political paradigms, left modern humanity with new emotions about itself and the world and human community. Modernity requires speed, passion, zeal, and magnetism. It stirs up, shouts louder, and pushes forward. It melts down and surges on, sweeping everything along with it, unlike the Oxford of the scholar's youth, which, lost in the pleasant dreams of academic pursuits, had "nothing of the beast" because it was "not built for gross, material gains."

---

[33]Lewis, "De Descriptione Temporum," 7.

CHAPTER FOUR

EVIL ENCHANTMENT

Psychology and Pedagogy in the Flatland

> *One understands a word much better if one*
> *has met it alive, in its native habitat.*
>
> C. S. LEWIS, STUDIES IN WORDS

> *The beauties which [poets of the Sixteenth Century] chiefly*
> *regarded . . . were those which we either dislike or simply*
> *do not notice. This change of taste makes an*
> *invisible wall between us and them.*
>
> C. S. LEWIS,
> ENGLISH LITERATURE IN THE SIXTEENTH CENTURY

IN HIS 1979 ESSAY "STANDING BY WORDS," the plainspoken farmer, poet, novelist, and essayist from Kentucky, Wendell Berry, declared that there are "two epidemic illnesses in our time—upon both of which virtual industries of cures have been founded": "the disintegration of communities and the disintegration of persons."[1] That seems

---

[1]Wendell Berry, *Standing by Words* (Berkeley, CA: Counterpoint, 1983), 24.

obvious enough. But Berry's next claim is deeper and, if true, more disturbing: "What seems not so well understood, because not so much examined, is the relation between these disintegrations and the dis-integration of language."[2] Berry illustrates the connection between dis-integration of language and disintegration of persons and community through an analysis of an official report on the Three Mile Island crisis, whose words are, in his opinion, "remarkable, and frightening." He found the report disturbing because the language within the document was marked by an "inability to admit what it is talking about. Because these specialists have routinely eliminated themselves, as such and as representative human beings, from consideration . . . they cannot bring themselves to acknowledge to each, much less to the public, that their problem involves an extreme danger to a lot people."[3] In other words, in Berry's critique, it is possible for a culture to become blind to moral responsibility, to lose a sense of courage and clarity, because it has become trapped within its own way of speaking. Certain fundamental, interior, and virtuous responses are suffocated because they do not have the linguistic atmosphere and habitat they need to flourish.

Decades earlier, C. S. Lewis anticipated Berry's insight, although he added one more factor to his analysis: it is not just that our ethics and our language are connected (Lewis agreed with this) but also that both language and ethics are connected to our cosmic imaginary. Our speech makes up a linguistic microcosm, the medium through which we describe our hopes, fears, dreams, and ambitions, and as such it absorbs and reflects the atmosphere of the world in which it is shaped. It was for this reason that he made the curious choice for his scholarly book *English Literature in the Sixteenth Century* to translate all of his quotations from Renaissance Latin authors into a mock, sixteenth-century English of his own devising, "not simply for the fun of it but to guard the reader from a false impression he might otherwise receive."[4]

---

[2]Berry, *Standing by Words*, 24.

[3]Berry, *Standing by Words*, 38.

[4]C. S. Lewis, *English Literature in the Sixteenth Century* (Oxford: Oxford University Press, 1954), v.

Lewis felt keenly the different atmospheres between the old ceremonial, courtly, baroque, artistic language of the premodern world, and our language, which is antipathetical to rhetoric and impatient with artificiality. There is an invisible wall between us and them:

> We must picture them growing up from boyhood in a world of "prettie epanorthosis," *paranomasia, isocolon,* and *similiter cadentia.* Nor were these, like many subjects in a modern school, things dear to the masters but mocked or languidly regarded by the parents. Your father, your grown-up brother, your admired elder schoolfellow, all loved rhetoric. Therefore, you loved it, too. You adored sweet Tully and were as concerned about asyndeton and chiasmus as a modern schoolboy is about country cricketers, or types of aeroplane.[5]

We prefer Hemingway to the baroque syntax of Milton. And yet, at the same time that this older English cultivated these elaborate, cosmological conventions through its high rhetoric, there was also a sense for the weightiness of everyday things:

> But against what seems to us this fantastic artificiality in their education we must set the fact that every boy, out of school, without noticing it, then acquired a range of knowledge such as no boy has today; farriery, forestry, archery, hawking, sowing, ditching, thatching, brewing, baking, weaving, and practical astronomy. This concrete knowledge, mixed with their law, rhetoric, theology, and mythology, bred an outlook very different from our own. High abstractions and rarified artifices jostled with the earthiest particulars. They would have found it very hard to understand the modern educated man who, though "interested in astronomy," knows neither who the Pleiades were nor where to look for them in the sky.[6]

In a paradoxical way, language in the old world was both more abstract and more concrete. Real things, better understood and encountered

---

[5]Lewis, *English Literature,* 61.
[6]Lewis, *English Literature,* 62.

on a daily basis, called forth a range of moral commitments that a mere economic object cannot. At the same time, the abstract terms possessed a weight, a density, a reality, in part because they were being "jostled" about with the "earthiest particulars."

The differences between linguistic styles from age to age are of interest precisely because we carry our "world" about within our language. Languages are subworlds, sharing similar deep structures to the universe in which they are native. Different languages vary in "tone and rhythm and the very 'feel' of every sentence,"[7] possessing their own "personalities,"[8] made up of unique syntaxes, vocabularies, and rhetorical styles: "A language has its own personality; implies an outlook, reveals a mental activity, and has a resonance, not quite the same as any other. Not only the vocabulary—*heaven* can never mean quite the same as *ciel*—but the very shape of the syntax is *sui generis*."[9] The uniqueness of language is due, in part, to the "world picture" that serves as the habitat in which that language is born, develops, and adapts. The cosmos gets into the language, like rainwater seeps into subterranean aquafers and regulates the height of the water table.

Because of this connection between language and world picture (what I have been calling, "cosmic imaginary"), not only should we expect language to change from age to age, but we should also expect that on this side of the Great Divide—the fundamental rupture in history that rendered modern society radically different from any other epoch in human history—the linguistic world we live in is peculiarly ill-suited to spiritual desire. As Lewis puts it in *The Abolition of Man*, the modern world is peculiarly arid, a "desert" not a "jungle."[10] This is also what Lewis was getting at when he referred to the "evil enchantment" of modernity.

---

[7]*DI*, 7.
[8]*DI*, 6.
[9]*DI*, 7.
[10]C. S. Lewis, *The Abolition of Man* (New York: Touchstone, 1996), 27.

The Evil Enchantment of the Modern World

As we've already seen in a previous chapter, Lewis anticipated contemporary historians of science by decades in espousing that over the course of centuries, changes in our external world picture (the so-called "mechanization of the world picture") was slowly internalized. According to Lewis, it even came to make up the very linguistic fabric of our minds. But what happens when the mechanized world picture becomes so obvious, such a part of the structures of our mind, that we cannot remember, or even imagine, an alternative? Lewis had a special name for this condition: "evil enchantment."

As a young man, he felt the pull of the spiritual world but, raised within the intellectual confines of modernity, he had no vocabulary that would allow him to take that quiet, whispering voice seriously, to understand it as anything but nostalgia. In his famous sermon "The Weight of Glory," Lewis reflects on such "enchantment":

> In speaking of this desire for our own far-off country, which we find in ourselves even now, I feel a certain shyness. I am almost committing an indecency. I am trying to rip open the inconsolable secret in each one of you—the secret which hurts so much that you take your revenge on it by calling it names like Nostalgia and Romanticism and Adolescence; the secret also which pierces with such sweetness that when, in very intimate conversation, the mention of it becomes imminent, we grow awkward and affect to laugh at ourselves; the secret we cannot hide and cannot tell, though we desire to do both. . . . The books or the music in which we thought the beauty was located will betray us if we trust to them; . . . . they are not the thing itself; they are only the scent of a flower we have not found, the echo of a tune we have not heard, news from a country we have never yet visited. Do you think I am trying to weave a spell? Perhaps I am; but remember your fairy tales. Spells are used for breaking enchantments as well as for inducing them. And you and I have need of the strongest spell that can be found to wake us from the

evil enchantment of worldliness which has been laid upon us for nearly a hundred years.[11]

These words about "evil enchantment" were published in 1941. Three years later, in *The Abolition of Man*, Lewis returned to the metaphors of enchantment and suppression, when he argued that "almost our whole education has been directed to silencing this shy, persistent, inner voice; almost all our modern philosophies have been devised to convince us that the good of man is to be found on this earth."[12] He returned to the theme of spells and forgetfulness again a decade later, in 1953, in *The Silver Chair*. Once the three travelers from Narnia Jill, Eustace, and Puddleglum have traveled deep underground, into the dark kingdom of a sorceress who holds a Narnian prince captive by an evil spell, the travelers, too, almost succumb to her bewitching enchantment. At one point, she realizes she has one last opportunity to try to enslave them all by casting yet a new spell of forgetfulness. The following passage echoes comments from both "The Weight of Glory" and *The Abolition of Man*:

> The witch said nothing at all, but moved gently across the room. . . . She took out a musical instrument rather like a mandolin. She began to play it with her fingers—a steady, monotonous thrumming that you didn't notice after a few minutes. But the less you noticed it, the more it got into your brain and your blood. This also made it hard to think. . . . After she had thrummed for a time . . . she began speaking in a sweet, quiet voice.
>
> "Narnia?" she said. "Narnia? I have often heard your Lordship utter that name in your ravings. Dear Prince, you are very sick. There is no land called Narnia."

---

[11]C. S. Lewis, "The Weight of Glory," *The Weight of Glory: And Other Addresses* (New York: HarperOne, 1980), 30-31.

[12]Lewis, *Abolition of Man*, 99. Alister McGrath's "Lewis's Philosophical Context at Oxford in the 1920's," in *The Intellectual World of C. S. Lewis* (London: Wiley-Blackwell, 2013), 31-54, provides a great sketch of the naturalism, reductivism, atheism, materialism, and "chronological snobbery" that dominated the intellectual world the young Lewis lived in, and thus why one would feel "shy" to admit such longings.

"Yes there is, though, Ma'am," said Puddleglum. "You see, I happened to have lived there all my life."

"Indeed," said the Witch. "Tell me . . . where that country is?"

"Up there," said Puddleglum, stoutly, pointing overhead. "I—I don't know exactly where."

"How?" said the Queen, with a kind, soft, musical laugh. "Is there a country up among the stones and mortar of the roof?"

"No," said Puddleglum, struggling a little to get his breath. "It's in Overworld."

"And what, or where, pray is this . . . how do you call it . . . *Overworld*?"

"Oh, don't be silly," said Scrubb, who was fighting hard against the enchantment. . . . "It's up above, up where you can see the sky and the sun and the stars. . . ."

"Please it your Grace," said the Prince. . . . "You see that lamp. It is round and yellow and gives light to the whole room; and hangeth moreover from the roof. Now that thing which we call the sun is like the lamp, only far greater and brighter. . . ."

"Hangest from what, my lord? . . . You see? When you try to think out clearly what this *sun* must be, you cannot tell me. You can only tell me it is like the lamp. Your *sun* is a dream; and there is nothing in that dream that was not copied from the lamp. The lamp is the real thing; the *sun* is but a tale, a children's story."[13]

Lewis was always reluctant to label fairy tales as literature for children. Here, through the medium of the fairy tale—that is, by looking "along" the beam—the professor of medieval literature explores what he had called in his nonfiction essays and sermons the evil enchantment of the modern world, the persistent attempt to suffocate the supernatural sentiments within. And we find him returning to this notion of enchantment yet again in "Transposition," where Lewis employs the image of drawing in linear perspective to illustrate the connection between the spiritual and physical worlds. He imagines engaging in

---

[13]C. S. Lewis, *The Silver Chair* (New York: HarperCollins, 1984), 173-75.

dialogue with a pert, two-dimensional figure, who lives in the two-dimensional plane of a drawing made in linear perspective. The two-dimensional figure is agnostic about the artist's "vaunted" three-dimensional world, and in expressing his doubt he echoes the witch's argument from *The Silver Chair*. The drawn figure might at first "be prepared to accept on authority our assurance that there was a world in three dimensions,"

> but when we pointed to the lines on the paper and tried to explain, say, that "This is a road," would he not reply that the shape which we were asking him to accept as a revelation of our mysterious other world was the very same shape which, on our own showing, elsewhere meant nothing but a triangle. And soon, I think, he would say, "You keep on telling me of this other world and its unimaginable shapes which you call solid. But isn't it very suspicious that all the shapes which you offer me as images or reflections of the solid ones turn out on inspection to be simply the old two-dimensional shapes of my own world as I have always known it? Is it not obvious that your vaunted other world, so far from being the archetype, is a dream which borrows all its elements from this one?"[14]

The two-dimensional figure doubts dimensions he cannot perceive; the witch tries to make the Narnians doubt that there even *is* an overworld; modernity casts a spell that makes those secret longings for a far-off country seem like mere emotions without a proper referent. Spiritual longing seems out of place in the modern world.[15]

Lewis also depicts this incongruity between "Old Western" and modernity in a conversation between Ransom and Merlin in *That Hideous Strength*. Merlin, the grave, unironic representative of the ancient

---

[14]C. S. Lewis, "Transposition," in *The Weight of Glory: And Other Addresses* (New York: HarperOne, 1980), 101.

[15]For the role of Plato in helping "awaken" Lewis from such spiritual somnolence, see Louis Markos, "C. S. Lewis's Christian Platonism," in *From Plato to Christ*, 202-13, as well as my "Evil Enchantment and the Platonic Vision: What Dante Taught Lewis About Poetry," *Sehnsucht*, vol. 11 (2017): 121-40.

pagan world, is confused and out of place in twentieth-century England. When Ransom has explained their dilemma, Merlin asks permission to "go in and out, and to and fro, renewing old acquaintances" with the land, to gather the needed herbs to serve as the instruments of his magic.[16] But Ransom strictly forbids it:

> "No," said the Director in a still louder voice, "that cannot be done any longer. The soul has gone out of the wood and water. Oh, I daresay you could awake them; a little. But it would not be enough. A storm, or even a river-flood would be of little avail against our present enemy. . . . Whatever of spirit may still linger in the earth has withdrawn fifteen hundred years further away from us since your time."[17]

In his conversation with Merlin, Ransom feels the chasm between them: "Merlin was like something that ought not to be indoors. Bathed and anointed though he was, a sense of mold, gravel, wet leaves, weedy water, hung about him."[18] In other words, the earth "tasted" differently in the age of Merlin, and so their vocabulary, modes of thinking, stylistic preferences are all at odds. And Lewis, the medievalist, cannot repress the detail that the old druid spoke a strange form of Latin, in an unfamiliar accent, with "a vocabulary that was far beyond [ordinary reading]—the Latin of a man whom Apuleius and Martianus Capella were the primary classics."[19]

In contrast to Merlin is the modern, midlevel bureaucrat, whose empty, hackneyed, dead professional prose is illustrative of the mechanized cosmos, a character the Oxford professor had fun skewering on more than one occasion. When the courtly King Caspian appears before Governor Gumpas in *The Voyage of the* Dawn Treader to rebuke him for allowing the slave trade to exist on his island, the old, tired, bureaucratic administrator gives a reply saturated in modern clichés: "An essential part of the economic development of the islands, I assure

---

[16]Lewis, *That Hideous Strength*, 285.
[17]Lewis, *That Hideous Strength*, 285-86.
[18]Lewis, *That Hideous Strength*, 285.
[19]Lewis, *That Hideous Strength*, 276.

you. Our present burst of prosperity depends on it. . . . Your Majesty's
tender years . . . hardly make it possible that you should understand
the economic problem involved. I have statistics, I have graphs, I
have . . ." Caspian interrupts:

> "Tender as my years may be . . . I do not see that it brings into the
> islands meat or bread or beer or wine or timber or cabbages or
> books or instruments of music or horses or armor or anything else
> worth having. But whether it does or not, it must be stopped."
>
>   "But that would be putting the clock back," gasped the gov-
> ernor. "Have you no idea of progress, or development?"[20]

Gumpas's speech is littered with abstractions, and abstractions of
things that have become more important than real things, real loves. He
feels some vague loyalty to hazy bureaucratic value words like *development* and *economic necessity*, terms that seem full of imperative urgency but have no power to evoke love for real, concrete things, in contrast to the Elizabethan schoolboy who knew and loved "farriery,
forestry, archery, hawking, sowing, ditching, thatching, brewing, baking,
weaving, and practical astronomy." No. Gumpas is a modern. He would
have loved to have helped us in our effort to flatten curves and social
distance. The language of Gumpas and other moderns, then, differs
from the linguistic world of the premodern age, in that it is simultaneously less concrete and less abstract. Gumpas doesn't believe in high
abstractions (like "Virtue," "Fate," "Judgment"), nor in earthly realities,
only in midlevel abstractions. Similarly, Uncle Andrew in *The Magician's Nephew* is also depicted as having no capacity to be attentive to
the harmonic chords that are building up the world before his eyes.
Present to the miracle of creation, he can only assess its potential economic value. Thoughts of beauty, wonder, and valor find no soil in the
dried-up language of his modern soul: "Stupendous, stupendous . . . I
have discovered a world where everything is bursting with life and
growth. Columbus, now, they talk about Columbus. But what was

---

[20]C. S. Lewis, *The Voyage of the* Dawn Treader (New York: HarperCollins, 1984), 49.

America to this? The commercial possibilities of this country are unbounded."[21]

Although the psychological and linguistic changes I have described took place first among the elite in the eighteenth and nineteenth centuries,[22] this way of viewing the world eventually worked its way all the way down into elementary-school textbooks, shaping anyone and everyone's perception of everyday life. This of course is exactly where *The Abolition of Man* begins.

IRRIGATING THE DESERT: MODERN EDUCATION IN A FLAT WORLD

The opening pages of *The Abolition of Man* deal with an incident in the life of the poet Samuel Taylor Coleridge, who once visited a waterfall and overheard two tourists. One called the waterfall "sublime," the other "pretty." Coleridge approved of the first, but the authors of the infamous *Green Book*, the elementary-school textbook Lewis analyzes in *The Abolition of Man*, are uninterested in that judgment of value. Rather, they intended to make a larger critical claim:

> When the man said, "this is sublime," he appeared to be making a remark about the waterfall. Actually, he was not making a remark about the waterfall, but a remark about his own feelings. What he was saying was really I have feelings associated in my mind with the word "sublime," or, shortly, I have sublime feelings. . . . This confusion is continually present in language as we use it. We appear to be saying something very important about something, and actually we are only saying something about our own feelings.[23]

In effect, Lewis argues, schoolchildren are implicitly taught that if they claim "that waterfall is sublime," they are making a worthless claim, because "I have sublime feelings about that waterfall" is

---

[21]C. S. Lewis, *The Magician's Nephew* (New York: HarperCollins, 1984), 120.
[22]See "Modern Man and His Categories of Thought," *EC*, 617.
[23]Lewis, *Abolition of Man*, 19.

merely a subjective assertion. And so, the schoolchild is silently led
to hold two propositions: "That all sentences containing a predicate
of value are statements about the emotional state of the speaker, and,
secondly, that all such statements are unimportant."[24] This is the
swollen, gorged Subject. All meaning lies within when the universe
has been emptied.

Lewis continues his exploration of how far into popular culture the
process of disenchantment has extended itself, referring to a second
example where the authors of the elementary textbook analyze a ba-
thetic advertisement for a cruise ship. In order to liberate their pupils
from the incantation of advertisement and other forms of mass propaganda, the authors of the textbook point out how factually inac-
curate the promises of the advertisement are. Lewis has no problem
with the authors exposing sentimental claims as shallow, but he also
thinks that these modern schoolmasters miss a great opportunity. If
these educators

> were to stick to their last and teach their readers (as they
> promised to do) the art of English composition, it was their
> business to put this advertisement side by side with passages
> from great writers in which the very same emotion is well
> expressed, and then show where the difference lies.
>
> They might have used Johnson's famous passage from the
> *Western Islands*, which concludes: "That man is little to be envied,
> whose patriotism would not gain force upon the plain of Mar-
> athon, or whose piety would not grow warmer among the ruins
> of Iona." They might have taken that place in *The Prelude* where
> Wordsworth describes how the antiquity of London first de-
> scended on his mind with "Weight and power, Power growing
> under weight." . . .
>
> The right defence against false sentiments is to inculcate just
> sentiments. By starving the sensibility of our pupils we only
> make them easier prey to the propagandist when he comes. . . .

---

[24]Lewis, *Abolition of Man*, 19.

Without the aid of trained emotions the intellect is power-
less against the animal organism.[25]

Thus, Lewis's critique is meant to expose how the authors' implicit
understanding of the world (as mechanized and quantified) affects
their pedagogy. As modern educators they feel it would be pedagogically dishonest to do anything but teach their students how to sift
through opinions in order to find facts, how to "debunk" myths. And
this stands in contrast to a premodern education, which was concerned with "inculcat[ing] just sentiments," enabling future genera-
tions to enter into harmony with the longings of the universe. Lewis's
opinion on the ethical consequences of such a transformation in
pedagogy was not ambiguous. If we are always standing back, keeping
the world at a distance to analyze, categorize, and quantify its parts,
then we will forever be in the position of looking "at" the beam. And
if that is the case, then we will lack the spiritual resource of the "heart,"
which must aid the reason to make for a fully-formed human being.
But modern education divorces the heart and mind, and the consequences are fatal, literally: "In a sort of ghastly simplicity we remove
the organ and demand the function. We make men without chests and
expect of them virtue and enterprise. We laugh at honour and are
shocked to find traitors in our midst. We castrate and bid the geldings
to be fruitful."[26]

Not so in the Long Middle Ages. Because they recognized that
"reason and appetite must not be left facing one another across a no-
man's land," their educational endeavors were directed to training sentiments such as "honor and chivalry" in order to provide the "'mean'

---

[25]Lewis, *Abolition of Man*, 21, 27, 35.

[26]Lewis, *Abolition of Man*, 36-37. "In battle it is not syllogisms that will keep the reluctant
nerves and muscles to their post. . . . We were told it all long ago by Plato. As the king
governs his executives, so Reason in man must rule the mere appetites by means of the
'spirited element.' The head rules the belly through the chest, the seat, as Alanus tells us,
of Magnanimity, of emotions organized by trained habit into stable sentiments. The
Chest—Magnanimity—Sentiment—these are indispensable liaison officers between cerebral man and visceral man. It may even be said that it is by this middle element that
man is man" (*Abolition of Man*, 35-36).

that unites them and integrates the civilized man."[27] And so, unlike modern attempts to create fact checkers and problem solvers and critical thinkers, Lewis's beloved old authors tried to model, inspire, and foster the just sentiments of piety, reverence, justice, and wonder. At the beginning of Dante's *Comedy*, the pilgrim, having just escaped from a bewildering and terrifying wood, sees a man in the path and calls out for help, but when he learns that the man standing before him is one of the venerable, old authors, he is immediately struck with a sense of shame, at being in the presence of his better, and reverence for the source of such wisdom. He exclaims,

> "Are you, then, Virgil? That spring and font
>   which gushed forth in a broad river of speech?"
> I said this, and said it with a humbled brow.
>
> "O! Pride and light of all poets,
>   let my long study and great love be merit for me,
> It was love that drove me to search through your tome.
>
> "You, you are my master! You are my authoritative guide!
> You are the only from whom I drew
> My beautiful style, the one who has brought me fame."[28]

Dante's immediate, natural, and heartfelt response of commitment, dedication, and loyalty is one of the many "just sentiments" (here, piety) that medieval educators hoped to instill into the hearts of their pupils. But there were others. Elsewhere we find Hugh of Saint Victor, for example, in his short treatise (*On the Three Days*) trying to elicit in his readers a rhapsodic admiration for the created universe. At one point in the treatise Hugh starts to heap up example after example, enthusiastically eulogizing the numerousness of things in the universe: "O how many things! How many there are! Count the stars of heaven, the sands of the sea, the dust of the earth, the drops of rain, the feathers of birds, the scales of fish, the hairs of animals, the grasses in fields, the

---

[27]*DI*, 58.
[28]Dante, *Inferno* 1.78-87, translation mine.

leaves and fruits of trees, and the innumerable number of innumerable other things!"[29]

In other words, for Hugh, it's not enough to provide students with the medieval equivalent of chemistry and physics; rather, we must come to the right sentiments of praise and admiration for creation. Similarly, Lewis was inspired by the gentle and frank Thomas Traherne, whose *Centuries* called (in a phrase that echoes Lewis's "just sentiments") for a "rendering to things their due esteem"[30]—that is, not just an understanding of the natural world but also a love and worshipful reverence for it. Traherne makes the argument that the greatest gift given to humankind is the natural world, and the appropriate way to receive it is, first, to study it, but then to wonder at it, to treasure it within, until you come to revere it: "The World is unknown, till the Value and Glory of it is seen: till the Beauty and the Serviceableness of its parts is considered. When you enter into it, it is an happy loss to lose oneself in admiration at one's own Felicity; and to find GOD in exchange for oneself. Which we then do when we see Him in His Gifts, and adore His Glory."[31] The human being coached and trained in the old education, then, was meant to have a whole range of just sentiments, like some kind of internal piano keyboard: a whole range of noble sentiments, ready to be played in response to the corresponding reality without, in lamentable contrast to the modern "trousered ape" and "urban blockhead" who have never been able "to conceive the Atlantic as anything more than so many million tons of cold salt water."[32] In other words, the spiritual children of Uncle Andrew.

Traditional education was as much an affair of the heart as of the mind, an inculturation into the way of honor, love, sacrifice, and integrity, as opposed to developing the thinking skills of Gumpas:

---

[29]Hugh of Saint Victor, *On the Three Days*, my translation, from the Latin text, *De Tribus Deibus*, ed. Dominique Poirel, Corpus Christinaorum. Continuatio Mediaevalis, CLXXVII (Turnhout, BE: Brepols Publishers, 2002), II.2. However, a complete English translation is available in *Trinity and Creation: A Selection of Hugh, Richard, and Adam of St. Victor*, ed. Boyd Coolman and Dale Coulter (Turnhout, Belgium: Brepols Publishers, 2010), 61-102.
[30]Lewis, *Abolition of Man*, 28.
[31]Thomas Traherne, *Centuries* (London: Harper, 1960), 1.18.
[32]Lewis, *Abolition of Man*, 23.

"Until quite modern times all teachers and even all men believed the universe to be such that certain emotional reactions on our part could be either congruous or incongruous to it—believed, in fact, that objects did not merely receive, but could *merit*, our approval or disapproval, our reverence, or our contempt."[33] And although Lewis found it laudable to equip students with precise powers of reasoning, so as to avoid being manipulated by the propaganda and advertisement of the modern world (which he loathed), he nevertheless believed that, in focusing on such concerns to the exclusion of training just sentiments, modern educators failed to note what their students actually need. We live in a spiritual desert, not a jungle:

> My own experience as a teacher tells an opposite tale. For every one pupil who needs to be guarded from a weak excess of sensibility there are three who need to be awakened from the slumber of cold vulgarity. The task of the modern educator is not to cut down jungles but to irrigate deserts. The right defence against false sentiments is to inculcate just sentiments. By starving the sensibility of our pupils we only make them easier prey to the propagandist when he comes.[34]

For all of these reasons, Lewis thought that chivalry, far from being some outdated, ritualistic social practice, was urgent again. Chivalry was the very endeavor to hold the parts of the human being in tension, to render a young man (in this case) an ethically whole person—that is, to unite those parts of a human being that do not naturally sit well with one another: extreme courage and gentle civility. It was no mistake that chivalry enjoyed its high noon in the age of the medieval model, whose polyphonic vision of the cosmos was analogous to a more complicated psychology, and yet, in "The Necessity of Chivalry," Lewis argues for the timeliness of such a morally ambitious project:

> The important thing about [the chivalric] is the double demand it makes on human nature. The knight is a man of blood and iron,

---

[33]Lewis, *Abolition of Man*, 29.
[34]Lewis, *Abolition of Man*, 27.

a man familiar with the sight of smashed faces and the ragged stumps of lopped-off limbs; he is also a demure, almost maiden-like, guest in hall, a gentle, modest, unobtrusive man. He is not a compromise or happy mean between ferocity and meekness; he is fierce to the *n*th and meek to the *n*th. . . . [Medieval chivalry] taught humility and forbearance to the great warrior because everyone knew by experience how much he usually needed that lesson. It demanded valor of the urbane and modest man because everyone knew that he was as likely as not to be a milksop.[35]

In conclusion, the premodern approach to the universe, and the ethical systems it constructed (chivalry), are of more than historical interest. Shifts in the tectonic plates of intellectual history altered the terrain of language; and the altered linguistic landscape created a world in which spiritual longing and just sentiments had come to feel out of place. This is Lewis's *ethical* defense of "Old Western": the old way of thinking about the world helped heal the "tragic dilemma" of being human. "As thinkers we are cut off from what we think about; as tasting, touching, willing, loving, hating, we do not clearly understand. The more lucidly we think, the more we are cut off: the more deeply we enter into reality, the less we can think." But Old Western, in its mythical approach to the world, provided a "partial solution" to this fragmentation, because "in the enjoyment of a great myth we come nearest to experiencing as a concrete what can otherwise be understood only as an abstraction. . . . Or, if you prefer, myth is the isthmus which connects the peninsular world of thought with the vast continent we really belong to."[36]

---

[35]C. S. Lewis, "The Necessity of Chivalry," in *Present Concerns*, ed. Walter Hooper (London: Harcourt Brace Jovanovich, 1986), 13-14.
[36]"Myth Became Fact," *EC*, 140-41.

CHAPTER FIVE

WHY LEWIS LOVED DANTE

Counterspells and the Weight of Glory

> *I think Dante's poetry, on the whole, the greatest of all the poetry I*
> *have read: yet when it is at its highest pitch of excellence, I hardly feel*
> *that Dante has very much to do. There is a curious feeling that the*
> *great poem is writing itself, or at most, that the tiny figure of the poet*
> *is merely giving the gentlest guiding touch, here and there, to energies*
> *which, for the most part, spontaneously group themselves and perform*
> *the delicate evolutions which make up the* Comedy.
>
> C. S. LEWIS, "DANTE'S SIMILES," *STUDIES IN MEDIEVAL*
> *AND RENAISSANCE LITERATURE*

BY THIS POINT WE HAVE SEEN that Lewis habitually contrasted our
modern cosmic imaginary, according to which the world is perceived
as a great, unintelligent, mechanistic, law-obeying, inert lump of mass,
with the medieval model, which combined "feeling" and "rationality,"
so much so that Lewis said we should think of the medieval picture of
the cosmos, not just as science, but simultaneously as art: "In speaking
of the perfected Model as a work to be set beside the *Summa* and the
Comedy, I meant that it is capable of giving a similar satisfaction to the
mind. . . . Like them [the Model] is vast in scale, but limited and

intelligible. Its sublimity is not the sort that depends on anything vague or obscure."[1] Given that the *universe* was felt to be a great poem or symphony, comparable to a medieval cathedral, Lewis, only half-humorously, suggested (cited in the epigraph to this chapter) that it must have been "easy" to write poetry in the Middle Ages. All you had to do was translate your "science" into verse. In Dante's cosmos there was less of a gap between metaphor and reality. For these reasons, Lewis felt Dante had special value for the modern world: he provided the model for how to speak of spiritual realities in a way in which they felt real, attractive, and weighty: in a phrase, he wrote a poetry that communicated the "weight of glory."

Perpetual Negations and Counterspells

In Christian theology, God and his heaven are rightly said to be timeless, spaceless, unable to be smelled, unable to be heard or seen. In this instance, though, correct theology presents a difficulty to the modern believer, as Lewis puts it in "Transposition": "Our notion of Heaven involves perpetual negations; no food, no drink, no sex, no movement, no mirth, no events, no time, no art."[2] Good Christians do, of course, believe that the vision of God will "outweigh" all these earthly affections, but Lewis worried that "our present notion" of the beatific vision cannot "outweigh our present notion" of the earthly goods we love:

> The negatives have, so to speak, an unfair advantage in every competition with the positive. What is worse, their presence—and most when we most resolutely try to suppress or ignore them—vitiates even such a faint and ghostlike notion of the positive as we might have had. The exclusion of the lower goods begins to seem the essential characteristic of the higher good. We feel, if we do not say, that the vision of God will come not to fulfill but to destroy our nature; this bleak fantasy often underlies our very use of such words as "holy" or "pure" or "spiritual."[3]

---

[1] *DI*, 12.
[2] "Transposition," in *The Weight of Glory: And Other Addresses* (New York: HarperOne, 1980), 107.
[3] Lewis, "Transposition," 108.

In other words, for most modern believers our image of heaven is watery, sallow, remote, shadowy, and faint. It doesn't have any "weight" or gravity or thickness (or "atmosphere"), and thus we often don't feel a positive attraction to goodness.

For this reason Lewis admired medieval literature, because he thought the old poems admirably created positive, heavy, sensuous images that gave weight in the imagination to elusive spiritual realities. For instance, in his *Allegory of Love*, as we have seen, Lewis praises the description of the garden in the medieval poem *Romance of the Rose*: "No one who remembers the fatuity of most poetical attempts to describe heaven—the dull catalogues of jewelry and mass-singing—will underrate this green park, its endless sunshine and fresh grass and grazing flocks."[4] Although medieval writers were as aware as we are of the limitations of their images (that is, they did not believe their metaphors were speaking any literal reality about spiritual truths), they were nevertheless willing to devote significant effort to trying to use positive pictures as symbols and "transpositions" of heavenly realities.[5] And this medieval awareness of the task of "transposition" could serve as a guide to modern writers. Dante could teach modern writers how to cast one of those "spells . . . used for breaking enchantments," as he put it in his "Weight of Glory" sermon, adding, "And you and I have need of the strongest spell that can be found to wake us from the evil enchantment of worldliness which has been laid upon us for nearly a hundred years."[6] And it was Dante more than any other author who taught Lewis about how to "build" images of weight that could allude to the dynamic truth of spiritual realities. Dante taught him how an artist could cast a "counterspell" in which the good feels weighty and attractive, a spell to overcome the "evil enchantment" cast by modernity.

---

[4]C. S. Lewis, *The Allegory of Love* (Oxford: Oxford University Press, 1958), 153.

[5]On this point, he agreed with his friend Owen Barfield. See Barfield's "The Texture of Medieval Thought," in *Saving the Appearances: A Study in Idolatry*, 2nd ed. (Hanover, NH: Wesleyan University Press, 1988), 84-91.

[6]C. S. Lewis, "The Weight of Glory," *The Weight of Glory: And Other Addresses* (New York: HarperOne, 1980), 31.

Although Lewis outgrew, for example, his admiration for Wordsworth, his admiration for the medieval Florentine poet Dante only increased from year to year. Dante's *Comedy*, in the assessment of Marsha Daigle-Williamson, is the single most important classic for "understanding Lewis's art," given that Lewis employs "Dante's masterpiece as the major literary model for his fiction."[7] The first instance we find of his reading Dante comes in 1917, when he took a seven-week crash course in Italian from Mr. Kirkpatrick. He reports proudly to his father, "On Sunday I read the first 200 lines of Dante with much success."[8] He read *Paradiso* over a happy vacation with his friend Owen Barfield, on which they divided their time between going for walks and reading passages from Dante in the afternoon, an experience he described to his friend Arthur Greeves. "Dante's *Paradiso*," he says,

> has really opened a new world to me. . . . It certainly seemed to me that I had never seen at all what Dante was like before. Unfortunately, the impression is one so unlike anything else that I can hardly describe it for your benefit—a sort of mixture of intense, even crabbed, complexity of language and thought with (what seems impossible) at the very same time a feeling of spacious gliding movement, like a slow dance, or like flying. It is like the stars—endless mathematical subtlety . . . yet at the same time the freedom and liquidity of empty space. . . . I should describe it as a feeling more important than any poetry I have ever read.[9]

In 1931 he read Dante every Thursday night with a fellow Oxford don.[10] Later, he became friends with Dorothy Sayers, and critiqued her

---

[7]Marsha Daigle-Williamson, *Reflecting the Eternal: Dante's "Divine Comedy" in the Novels of C. S. Lewis* (Peabody, MA: Hendrickson, 2015), 201.

[8]*Letters*, 1:275.

[9]*Letters*, 1:857. The following summer he added, "Barfield and I finished the *Paradiso* when I was with him. I think it reaches heights of poetry which you get nowhere else: an ether almost too fine to breathe. It is a pity that I can give you no notion what it is like. Can you imagine Shelley at his most ecstatic combined with Milton at his most solemn and rigid? It sounds impossible I know, but that is what Dante has done" (July 8, 1930, *Letters*, 1:915).

[10]See his letter to his brother, November 22, 1931, *Letters*, 2:16.

translation of the *Comedy* as she produced it, one canto at a time. In his three most important scholarly books, Lewis refers to Dante around seventy times, as if his mind were constantly drifting back to the Italian poet as the official standard of measurement for all premodern literature.[11] In *The Problem of Pain*, he cites Dante's description of the god of love as an example of the numinous. For *The Great Divorce* he confessed to borrowing multiple passages from Dante, and he also admitted to a scholar that his Green Lady in *Perelandra* was modeled on Dante's Matelda.[12] And, as we have seen, Lewis's mind returned to Dante in times of grief. There doesn't seem to be a moment in Lewis's adult life in which Dante was not close at hand and vividly present in his thoughts. The Florentine was a constant interlocutor. Just as when Augustine wanted to talk about love or loss, and would reach into his mind to try to find language adequate to capture the power of the experience, and would inadvertently begin quoting passages from Virgil, Lewis would open his mouth to say something moving and personal and find himself quoting Dante.[13]

What was it in Dante, then, that compelled such strong affection? We have already seen the first part of Lewis's answer to this question: the medieval poet was the beneficiary of living in a cosmos that was inherently poetic. Many of those instances where Dante seems very poetical in our eyes, advancing daring metaphors, Lewis contests, are not actually very inventive at all. Dante was only giving voice to medieval "science."

But the second reason his poetry exerted such an influence over Lewis's imagination takes us back to the idea of transposition, the metaphor Lewis used to describe the dynamic in which a higher language finds expression within a lower one. Dante the dreamer, the visionary, the lover, engaged in a restless struggle throughout his life to find sensible imagery for invisible, placeless, timeless events. As a

---

[11]For an extensive list of all such references, see Daigle-Williamson, *Reflecting the Eternal*.

[12]For Dante and *The Great Divorce*, see his letter of July 30, 1954, *Letters*, 3:498.

[13]For Augustine, see Sabine MacCormack, *The Shadows of Poetry: Vergil in the Mind of Augustine* (Berkeley, CA: University of California Press, 1998).

young poet, writing love lyric, he sought to describe the elusive nature of love. As a slightly older poet, writing his *Vita Nuova*, he sought to describe the movement of love toward transcendent beauty. And as a mature poet, in his masterpiece, he sought to describe guilt, hatred, freedom, desire for virtue, love of neighbor, holiness, and the ineffable majesty of God. But he always did so through famously and sometimes shockingly palpable imagery: decapitated troubadours, sinners who scream at God, blind beggars leaning on one another's shoulders for support, or the souls on Saturn buzzing around like tops to express their joyful zeal. In Lewis's words, the chief characteristic of Dante's poetry is its "almost sensuous intensity about things not sensuous."[14] In contrast to the "dull catalogues of jewelry and mass-singing,"[15] Dante's poetry gets *more* concrete, more sensible, more tangible, with every step closer toward God. Even when treating the most abstract realities of all, we have images of

> Dante in the garden, and Dante in the streets, his feeling for the silent growing life, and his cheerful, spontaneous interest in the state and courtesies, the trades and skills, of men. It is, perhaps, this continual reference both to the quiet, moistened earth and to the resonant pavements, workshops, and floors, which support and make convincing his invention of a heaven which, in the obvious sense, makes very few concessions to the natural man.[16]

Indeed, Lewis was so interested in the particulars of how Dante built this earthy atmosphere into his poetry—or what he had called "a sort of mixture of intense, even crabbed, complexity of language" with a "spacious gliding movement"[17]—that he undertook a study to tally all of the metaphors and similes in the last eleven canti of *Paradiso*—that is, those most abstract parts of Dante's poem. Having made a catalog of all the imagery, Lewis divided the images up into different

---

[14]C. S. Lewis, "Imagery in the Last Eleven Cantos of Dante's 'Comedy,'" in *Medieval and Renaissance Literature*, Canto Classics (Cambridge: Cambridge University Press, 1998), 93.
[15]Lewis, *Allegory of Love*, 153.
[16]Lewis, "Imagery," 93.
[17]*Letters*, 1:857.

categories. And the results of the lists are more fascinating than you would think! According to Lewis's reckoning, there are three images and metaphors that refer to smells; two images for pressing seals in wax; two metaphors borrowed from the life of the student; four images that use the metaphor of sleep and waking to describe how Dante reacted to some heavenly phenomenon. Then there are five images of children, mainly of infants nursing. When we remember that Dante was a love poet, it comes as a surprise that there are only seven metaphors that refer to marriage or erotic love. On the other hand, it is surprising that we have seven images for "weighing" or "weight": as Lewis puts it, "I have always felt that no poetry—least of all, any poet whose theme is so unearthly as Dante's—has such an admirable solidity."[18] This class is particularly exemplary because Lewis's favorite Dantean image belongs to it. When Dante is being examined by Saint James on the virtue of hope in *Paradiso* 25, the pilgrim, like a student taking a very difficult oral exam, looks up in search of comfort and encouragement from his professor. The poet describes this gaze as similar to when one looks up at nearby mountains, which do not just seem high, but dizzying, as if they were exerting weight merely by being so high. When Dante gazes at the saintly figures, he feels their "heavy" holiness, as weighty as the mass of mountains. And here we have Dante at his best (in Lewis's opinion): that intangible, saintly glory is portrayed as with crushing density, pressing in and down on you, as if you were at the bottom of the sea: "No direct praise of their wisdom or sanctity could have made us respect them half so much."[19] I have argued elsewhere that when Lewis preached his famous "Weight of Glory" sermon on 2 Corinthians 4:17 ("For our light affliction, which is but for a moment, worketh for us a far more exceeding and eternal weight of glory") he had this bit of poetry from Dante in mind. The Florentine poet helped the medieval scholar gloss Scripture.[20]

---

[18]Lewis, "Imagery," 84.

[19]Lewis, "Imagery," 80.

[20]Jason M. Baxter, "Evil Enchantment and the Platonic Vision: What Dante Taught Lewis About Poetry," *Sehnsucht*, vol. 11 (2017): 121-40.

But there are also astronomical and military references; nine images of clothing, and not just the "white robes and golden crowns" you might expect; rather, we hear of how joy "wraps" Adam up as if he were swaddled in a blanket: "[Dante's] mind . . . is apparently very sensitive to the experience of putting on, being enfolded, swathed, enveloped."[21] There are also nine metaphors that refer to tying up or binding with rope, as well as images of smiling, laughter, and even wounds, such as references to how "love" bites with many teeth. Lewis goes on to add twelve metaphors that refer to the opening and closing of things; sixteen zoological metaphors (especially birds); twenty-four for weather, such as dawns and dew, sunrises and plentiful rain; twenty-four more for civic functions (such as likening the saints to barons, or the communion of saints to a city); twenty-five images of light and heat; and twenty-five images of plants and vegetation. "The poetry of *Paradiso* is as full of roots and leaves and growth as it is of lights."[22] And finally, the image that occurs more than any other, those that pertain to trades and crafts:

> The arts, crafts, manufacturers, and skilled occupations of men: from painting, musical instruments, seals and sealing-wax, clocks, thread, money in a purse, hammer and anvil, rowing, riddling with a sieve, archery at the butts, the cares of the artist, the jeweller, the geometrician and the astronomer observing an eclipse, and finally (on the very eve of the ineffable vision) a prudent reminder that a good tailor cuts his coat according to his cloth.[23]

In light of Lewis's lists of Dante's images, we can begin to see Dante through Lewis's eyes. We can see why reading the *Paradiso* felt, to the youthful Lewis, like joining in some "spacious gliding movement, like a slow dance, or like flying." It was ethereal, but at the same time tactile and tangible and sensuous and palpable. Dante's language constantly

---

[21]Lewis, "Imagery," 85.
[22]Lewis, "Imagery," 90.
[23]Lewis, "Imagery," 92.

evokes ordinary, terrestrial events, daily crafts, and diurnal happenings—such as growth, and eating, and clothing. Dante uses concrete and humble things even when gesturing, in wonder, at that distant country of heaven. In other words, Lewis loved Dante because he made his heaven envelop, penetrate, invade, burn, and restlessly seek to come within.[24]

But Dante didn't just sprinkle similes throughout his poem. In certain passages, the poet heaps them up and piles them together, in bravura moments of poetic composition. Toward the end of *Paradiso*, for example, there is one scene in particular (*Paradiso* 30–31) that illustrates the medieval poet's delight in stacking up image upon image, creating a kaleidoscopic poetry that gives a dizzying sensation of exhilaration. There Dante the pilgrim sees, for the first time, the whole community of saints gathered in one great assembly. Up until this point, he has had conversations with individuals, but without being able to contextualize them within the whole. But now, the pilgrim stares, mesmerized, at all of the saints gathered together. And as the pilgrim gazes, the poet desperately seeks a likeness or metaphor that will do justice to the spiritual radioactivity of their commingled glory. At first the poet likens them to a collection of flowers in a meadow, but he quickly switches to describing them as a single rose. He then drops that metaphor and likens the saints to a city, before turning to comparing them to an army, marching in rank and file. He returns to comparing them to petals on a white rose, before pulling out all the stops. Soon we hear of a river that shoots forth sparks and how those sparks leap out and fall on flowers, which are likened to "rubies inscribed in gold."[25] And then "the living sparks,"[26] as though inebriated by the odors of the flowers,[27] plunge back into the river.

---

[24]Compare Lewis's assessment of Dante with what he said about the education of sixteenth-century schoolboys, as cited above. *English Literature in the Sixteenth Century* (Oxford: Oxford University Press, 1954), 62.

[25]Dante, *Paradiso* 30.65-66. This and the following references to *Paradiso* are my translation.

[26]Dante, *Paradiso* 30.64.

[27]Dante, *Paradiso* 30.67.

Dante later likens this whole vision to a hill reflected in a body of water at its base, as if it were studying itself in a mirror.[28] The reality to which Dante gestures is ineffable; it eludes words, and thus this intensely shifting and undulating imagery is appropriate. The sliding metaphors employed create a dreamlike intensity, as if the poet were looking through a kaleidoscope. And yet, Beatrice says, "the river, the topazes / . . . the laughter of the meadows / *are shadowy prefaces of their truth*."[29] Dante's language is vibrantly alive, as if a higher mode of being were irrupting in a lower language, and as if, under high pressure, the lower language were melting down. This is what Lewis identifies as Dante's "intensity of thought": Dante simultaneously combines "weight" and "soaring," and thus paradoxically renders sensible that which is beyond language. This is a good example of how a poet performs "transposition."

There's a third feature of Dante's poetry Lewis admired: Dante's fidelity to the past. He was what Lewis called a maker of "traditional poetry." He restored, reused, recycled, and revitalized old dead metaphors. For example, everyone knows how Paul calls the Christian a "new creation" (2 Cor 5:17), but Dante newly imagines that tired metaphor in his poetry. The saints in heaven, as they are variously described in *Paradiso,* shine brighter than stars, move more swiftly than lightning, produce a more lovely harmony than the planets, glow like an unending sunrise, smile more radiantly than the sun, rush swifter than cold, mountain winds. Each saint outdoes, as it were, the entirety of the old celestial order. A saintly soul is a new creation, and the re-creation of a human being is as dramatic an event as God's creation of the first cosmos.[30] It was this talent for rehabilitating dead metaphors that Lewis admired in Dante (and other medieval authors). He loved poets "who have at once the tenderest care for old words and the surest instinct for the creation of

---

[28]Dante, *Paradiso* 30.110-11.

[29]Dante, *Paradiso* 30.76-78.

[30]For more on this "cosmological" element of holiness in the mind of Dante, see my *Infinite Beauty of the World: Dante, Medieval Encyclopedism, and the Names of God,* Leeds Dante Series (Oxford: Peter Lang, 2020).

new metaphors."[31] As we have seen, in his preaching and fiction, Lewis attempted something similar.

In short, then, Lewis admired Dante's poetry for its indebtedness to the medieval cosmos; for how it tried to work into sensible, and even humble, imagery that which is beyond words (its "sacramental" or "symbolic" character); and how the great poet humbly borrowed old (formerly cliched) metaphors but managed to revitalize them. We have to keep this analysis in mind when turning to Lewis's own fiction.

THE NEW DANTE

Lewis took this special, metaphorical sensuousness as a guiding principle for his own imaginative writing. As we have seen, Lewis felt that the fairy tale provided him with the medium he needed to help reverse the religious coldness he had experienced in his own childhood.[32] And so, following his medieval exemplars, Lewis adopted an imaginative dream-fiction of great plasticity for *The Great Divorce*, a work heavily indebted to Dante. Lewis begins the story with a confused, first-person narration about a man (we later realize it is "Lewis" himself, analogous to Dante the poet's use of "Dante-the-pilgrim") walking around an eerily discourteous and empty city over the course of an evening that never turns to night (an attempt to re-create Dante-pilgrim's experience in the dark wood in *Inferno* 1). This modern pilgrim boards a bus that takes off in a magical flight. Lewis's angelic driver is dismissive and disdainful, just as the angelic messenger is in *Inferno* 9. And when the bus arrives in heaven, the curious tourists are allowed to explore and hold conversations with loved ones from earth, who, now heavenly saints, use every honest rhetorical trick available to appeal to their freedom, urging them to surrender, confess, and stay. This, too, is modeled on Dante-pilgrim's series of successive conversations with souls in the afterlife. There are also vague prophecies about future darkness, which directly parallel the prophecies of the souls in

---

[31]C. S. Lewis, "Bluspels and Flanasferes," in *Selected Literary Essays*, ed. Walter Hooper, Canto Classics (Cambridge: Cambridge University Press, 2013), 265.
[32]See "Sometimes Fairy Stories May Say Best What's to Be Said," *EC*, 526-29.

hell who tell Dante that a day will come in which they will be able to see no more and darkness will enclose them.[33] Finally, Lewis's interaction with his teacher George MacDonald parallels the instruction that Dante receives from Virgil and other guides, while the scene in which MacDonald tells Lewis to "tell the truth plainly" echoes in particular the frank advice that Dante's great-great-grandfather Cacciaguida gives him in *Paradiso* 15–17. Lewis also borrows Dante's procession at the end of *Purgatorio*—when Beatrice, escorted by mythological animals, angels, and saints, makes her grand entry in *Purgatorio* 29—for his own depiction of the grand procession of the "ordinary" housewife, Sarah Smith.

But more important than such borrowings of detail or character is the whole poetic technique, the quest to get that "weighty" quality of goodness, the substantial heaviness of heavenly reality. *The Great Divorce* is a great metaphysical thought experiment, whose ingenious nature is only revealed at the very end. Throughout the story, Lewispilgrim has insinuated that he has doubts about the goodness of heaven. Doesn't heaven feel a bit snobbish? After all, if the saints are *so* loving, why wouldn't they be willing to leave their comfortable heavenly home and visit the damned in hell? When Lewis, toward the end of the story, expresses this very modern sentiment, his teacher gives "a curious smile," before replying as follows:

> "Look," he said, and with the word he went down on his hands and knees. I did the same . . . and presently saw that he had plucked a blade of grass. Using its thin end as a pointer, he made me see, after I had looked very closely, a crack in the soil so small that I could not have identified it without this aid.
>
> "I cannot be certain," he said, "that this *is* the crack ye came up through. But through a crack no bigger than that ye certainly came."
>
> "But-but," I gasped with a feeling of bewilderment not unlike terror. "I saw an infinite abyss. And cliffs towering up and up. And then *this* country on top of the cliffs."

---

[33]See, e.g., Dante, *Inferno* 6; 10.

"Aye. But the voyage was not mere locomotion. That bus, and all you inside it, were increasing *in size*."

"Do you mean that Hell—all that infinite empty town—is down in some little crack like this?"

"Yes. All Hell is smaller than one pebble of your earthly world: but it is smaller than one atom of *this* world, the Real World. . . ."

"It seems big enough when you're in it, Sir."

"And yet, all loneliness, angers, hatreds, envies and itchings that it contains, if rolled into one single experience and put into the scale against the least moment of the joy that is felt by the least in Heaven, would have no weight that could be registered at all."[34]

In this revelatory moment, then, Lewis reveals that his story is an imaginative vehicle—a modern fantasy story or fairy tale—devised to make a metaphysical (and medieval) point: in medieval thought pure evil is the same as nothingness, it's like absolute zero on the Kelvin scale. Ultimate happiness is, rather, ontological fullness. Pure concentrated joy. The simultaneous possession of the fullness of life. Such fullness makes evils deeds—which seem so threatening, enticing, alluring, and enchanting—seem pathetic and almost nonexistent by contrast. This is the poetic counterspell by which Lewis (and Dante before him) employed the flexible vehicle of myth in order to make us feel, even if just for a moment, the weight and heaviness of ultimate reality.

---

[34]C. S. Lewis, *The Great Divorce* (New York: MacMillan, 1978), 122-23.

CHAPTER SIX

HOW *to* PRAY *to* *a* MEDIEVAL GOD

C. S. Lewis and Mysticism

It is as hard to explain how this sunlit land was different from the old Narnia as it would be to tell you how the fruits of that country taste. Perhaps you will get some idea of it if you think like this. You may have been in a room in which there was a window that looked out on a lovely bay of the sea or a green valley that wound away among mountains. And in the wall of that room opposite there may have been a looking-glass. And as you turned away from the window you suddenly caught sight of that sea or that valley, or all over again, in the looking-glass. And the sea in the mirror, or the valley in the mirror, were in one sense just the same as the real ones: yet at the same time, they were somehow different—deeper, more wonderful, more like places in a story: in a story you have never heard but very much want to know. The difference between the old Narnia and the new Narnia was like that. The new one was a deeper country: every rock and flower and blade of grass looked as if it meant more. I can't describe it any better than that. If you ever get there, you will know what I mean.

C. S. LEWIS, *THE LAST BATTLE*

IN THE MAGNIFICENT FINAL CHAPTER OF *Voyage of the* Dawn Treader, "The Very End of the World," Lewis creates a narrative that is, paradoxically, both eerily still and dramatically energetic. Of all of Lewis's fiction, this chapter might have borrowed the most from Dante's *Paradiso*, given its emphasis on the constant increase of light and joy, which comes on in ever new waves, as the crew speeds toward the end of the world:

> Every day and every hour the light became more brilliant and still they could bear it. No one ate or slept and no one wanted to, but they drew buckets of dazzling water from the sea, stronger than wine and somehow wetter, more liquid, than ordinary water, and pledged one another silently in deep drafts of it. And one or two of the sailors who had been oldish men when the voyage began now grew younger every day. Everyone on board was filled with joy and excitement, but not an excitement that made one talk. The further they sailed the less they spoke, and then almost in a whisper. The stillness of that last sea laid hold on them.[1]

Things at the end of the world are more real: water is more wet, light more brilliant, humans less sluggish, in need of less nutrition and sleep. Communication, too, becomes easier. As they briskly sail along, the crew communicates *more* by speaking *less*. Intuition, nods, heartfelt gestures, and communion replace mere communication, such as when Lucy, within the span of a glance, strikes up a lifelong friendship with a creature from the sea: "Lucy had liked that girl and she felt certain the girl had liked her. In that one moment they had somehow become friends. There does not seem to be much chance of their meeting again in that world or any other. But if ever they do they will rush together with their hands held out."[2] The universe is starting to behave like it ought to.

The concluding chapter of *The Voyage of the* Dawn Treader also shares important similarities with the penultimate chapter of *The Last*

---

[1]C. S. Lewis, *The Voyage of the* Dawn Treader (New York: HarperCollins, 1984), 233-34.
[2]Lewis, *Voyage*, 233.

Battle, in which the fugitives from Narnia unexpectedly find themselves in Aslan's country. As they cautiously explore their new world,
they are continually surprised by how much it reminds them of the
old Narnia. Trying to orient themselves in this oddly familiar place,
the company keeps commenting on how this or that feature is both
like and unlike the world they had known (as cited in the epigraph to
this chapter), until finally the Unicorn is able to sum up what everyone
was feeling: "I have come at last! This is my real country! I belong here.
This is the land I have been looking for all my life, though I never knew
it till now. The reason why we loved the old Narnia is that it sometimes
looked a little like this."[3] In the passage leading up to the Unicorn's
excited cry (as cited in the epigraph to this chapter), we find that all of
those tellingly Platonic keywords, which Lewis explicated in his important "symbolism" passage in *Allegory of Love* (discussed above),
have made their fictional comeback: mirrors, reflections, images,
copies, and the contrast between flatness and depth. Indeed, at the end
of the world in *The Voyage of the* Dawn Treader or in Aslan's country
in *The Last Battle,* we enter into a landscape from which all shadows
and reflections are banished. Colors are brilliant again. And if there
was any doubt about Lewis's source, the old professor—Lord Diggory—
sets everyone straight:

> "Listen. . . . When Aslan said you could never go back to Narnia,
> he meant the Narnia you were thinking of. But that was not the
> real Narnia. That had a beginning and an end. It was only a
> shadow or a copy of the real Narnia which has always been here
> and always will be here: just as our own world, England and all,
> is only a shadow or copy of something in Aslan's real world. You
> need not mourn over Narnia, Lucy. All of the old Narnia that
> mattered, all the dear creatures, have been drawn into the real
> Narnia through the Door. And of course it is different; as dif-
> ferent as a real thing is from a shadow or as waking life is from
> a dream." His voice stirred everyone like a trumpet as he spoke

---

[3]C. S. Lewis, *The Last Battle* (New York: HarperCollins, 1984), 195-96.

these words: but when he added under his breath, "It's all in Plato, all in Plato."[4]

As Diggory's comments suggest, this no *mere* children's story. Indeed, it represents the fruit of thirty years of academic meditation on the symbolic nature of the medieval cosmos.

In his own hesitant way, Lewis is using his fiction to deal with mysticism, the quest to seek out that for which we barely have a name, to encounter God in the fullness of his glory, at the center of my heart. It is the satisfaction of the secret ache within (or what Lewis, in "The Weight of Glory," calls the "inner wound"). In both stories, it was a struggle to get there, but now that they have arrived at the end of the world or in Aslan's country, virtue yields to amazement, struggle against disorder yields to ecstatic rest. Goodness has become easy, and seeing is contemplative. All the travelers have to do is look around, drink in the beauty of the world, and rest in a landscape of joy. Once we are tuned into this semantic web of related key terms—flatness versus the multidimensional; "picture" or "portrait" or "mirror" versus the real landscape; the sharp and hot versus the bloodless, the cold, and the dull—we are in a position to see how ubiquitous the themes of "transposition" or "symbolism" (in Lewis's sense) or "sacramentalism" are in Lewis's imagination. Indeed, Lewis himself summed up the whole essence of the Christian life as turning "from the portraits to the Original, from the rivulets to the Fountain"![5]

THE DANGER OF MYSTICISM

This mystical impulse—this desire to look behind the veil of this world and speculate about what is behind—made up Lewis's spiritual DNA. Indeed, for both Lewis and Dante, the Christian life culminates in something higher than morality. At the highest level of spiritual perfection, there is a kind of play, a joyful unfolding of freedom. And so it might come as a surprise to find the writer constantly disavowing it,

---

[4]Lewis, *Last Battle*, 194-95.
[5]C. S. Lewis, *The Four Loves* (London: Fontana Books, 1960), 127.

pushing it away, and discouraging his friends and readers from trying to practice it. For example, in "The Weight of Glory," after soaring to incredible heights of theological speculation, he turns back, reins himself in, and warns people about getting carried away:

> What would it be to taste at the fountain-head that stream of which even these lower reaches prove so intoxicating? Yet that, I believe, is what lies before us. The whole man is to drink joy from the fountain of joy. As St. Augustine said, the rapture of the saved soul will "flow over" into the glorified body. In the light of our present specialized and depraved appetites we cannot imagine this *torrens voluptatis*, and I warn everyone seriously not to try.[6]

Likewise, in *The Four Loves*, when Lewis finally climbs the heights to discuss divine love, he breaks off his discussion after just one paragraph: "But all that is far away in 'the land of the Trinity,' not here in exile, in the weeping valley. Down here it is all loss and renunciation."[7] And, so too, in his personal letters, he often put distance between himself and mysticism. In one letter he disavowed being a mystic or being an academic authority on it.[8] Once, when writing to his friend and former student Bede Griffiths, having congratulated him on the publication of his new book *Christianity in India*, he sternly warned him, "You are (as you well know) on dangerous ground about Hinduism, but someone must go to dangerous places." Why the cautious reservation? Lewis explained, "Your Hindus certainly sound delightful. But what do they deny? That's always been my trouble with Indians— to find any proposition they wd. pronounce false. But truth must surely involve exclusions?"[9]

In other words, Lewis was pastorally and pedagogically hesitant about mysticism for two reasons. The first is that the more difficult task

---

[6]Lewis, "The Weight of Glory," 44.
[7]Lewis, *Four Loves*, 127.
[8]"Don't give him the illusion that I'm a mystic or an authority on mysticism" (April 25, 1953, *Letters*, 3:325).
[9]*Letters*, 3:1040-41.

for us human beings is the humbler and more regular one: being consistent, being faithful, acting with fortitude, and acting out obedience with alacrity, or as Lewis puts it, "Meanwhile the cross comes before the crown and tomorrow is a Monday morning."[10] The second reason for hesitance is Lewis's fear that mysticism—explained at length in *Miracles*, as we will see—could lead to a vague "spirituality," a misty belief in a "divine principle." By rendering God into a life force or "principle of happiness," I also effectively delete from my imagination "personality," that there is a God seeking *me*, and who wants me to live for him.[11] This personal accountability is more frightening because it makes concrete demands on my time, energy, and life, as opposed to some vague, uplifting sense of duty. In fact, Screwtape recommends such fuzzy "mystical" thinking as a way of distracting Christians: "That is exactly the sort of prayer we want; and since it bears a superficial resemblance to the prayer of silence as practised by those who are very far advanced in the Enemy's service, clever and lazy patients can be taken in by it for quite a long time."[12] A great strategy: make him a mystic, and land him in hell.

But even if Lewis had pastoral and pedagogical reservations about mystical practice, it would be a huge mistake to overlook the presence of mystical theology in Lewis's life, as David Downing has shown in his excellent book.[13] For every time that the inventor of Narnia puts distance between himself and mysticism, you can find five passages in which mysticism, as it were, "sneaks up" and is hiding just around the corner. Indeed, Lewis seems to have been following good mystical authority to warn his readers off of mysticism, not because he distrusted the old texts, but precisely because he was following their advice! At the beginning of *The Cloud of Unknowing*, we find the anonymous medieval author conducting what we would judge a terrible marketing campaign, urging his readers not to share or

---

[10]Lewis, "The Weight of Glory," 45.

[11]I discuss this in detail in chap. 7, "Deep Conversion and Unveiling," below.

[12]C. S. Lewis, *The Screwtape Letters* (New York: Scribner, 1996), 16.

[13]David C. Downing, *Into the Region of Awe: Mysticism in C. S. Lewis* (Downers Grove, IL: InterVarsity Press, 2005).

recommend the book with anyone. The fifteenth-century author gravely warns,

> I charge and beg you, with all the strength and power that love can bring to bear, that whoever you may be who possess this book (perhaps you own it, or are keeping it, carrying it, or borrowing it) you should, quite freely and of set purpose, neither read, write, or mention it to anyone, nor allow it to be read, written, or mentioned by anyone unless that person is in your judgement really and wholly determined to follow Christ perfectly. And to follow him not only in the active life, but to the utmost height of the contemplative life that is possible for a perfect soul in a mortal body to attain by the grace of God. And he should be, in your estimation, one who has for a long time been doing all that he can to come to the contemplative life by virtue of his active life. Otherwise the book will mean nothing to him.[14]

This counterintuitive advice is related to a standard teaching in the mystical tradition, that there are moral and spiritual stages of growth, which one must proceed through in the right order: Purification must precede illumination; and illumination precedes unity. For the medieval mind, you could not skip to the end: you *had* to be religious before being spiritual.

INTO THE CLOUD OF UNKNOWING

All the same, that did not mean that the Christian life was synonymous with moral rectitude. Indeed, perhaps no age of Christianity has been more aware of the difference between following a moral code and the real mystery of Christian religion. Medieval authors knew that the ultimate goal of the Christian life was not ethical, but to come to the point at which one loves God freely and unbounded. Such desire to be free of distorting and cramped love is well summarized in a medieval legend in which Christ appears to Thomas Aquinas, addressing him: "You have spoken well of me, Thomas. What is your reward to

---

[14]*Cloud of Unknowing*, trans. Clifton Wolters (London: Penguin Books, 1978), prologue, 51.

be?" Aquinas replies, "Nothing other than Thee, Lord!"[15] In a similar way, the author of the *Cloud*—a book that, as Downing points out, Lewis adored and often recommended—passionately describes that highest stage of the spiritual life, in which we come to desire "God himself, and not what you get out of him." Indeed, the anonymous author goes so far as to recommend that we "try to forget all created things that he ever made . . . so that your thought and longing do not turn or reach out to them either in general or in particular. Let them go, and pay no attention to them."[16] In the highest stages of mystical ascent, the soul tries to forget everything, even loved ones and theological doctrines, paring prayer sometimes down to a single syllable, repeating, over and over again, "God" or "sin." The soul repeats these expressions, but with longing and groaning, so as to get beyond them: "Why does it penetrate heaven, this short little prayer of one syllable? Surely because it is prayed with a full heart, in the height and depth and length and breadth of the spirit of him that prays it."[17]

The anonymous medieval author's potent metaphor for this type of wordless prayer is moving into a "dark cloud," in which God's light is hidden from our intellect by its brilliance. Our intellect is incapable of reaching out and understanding fully, so we have to be patient, standing in the dark, but continually reaching out and upward: "Reconcile yourself to wait in this darkness as long as is necessary, but still go on longing after him whom you love. For if you are to feel him or to see him in this life, it must always be in this cloud, in this darkness."[18]

The *Cloud of Unknowing*, as Lewis well knew, borrows its central metaphor—the dark cloud—from another one of Lewis's authors:

---

[15]Jean-Pierre Torrell, *St. Thomas Aquinas: The Person and His Works*, trans. Robert Royal (Washington, DC: Catholic University of America Press, 1996), 285.

[16]*Cloud of Unknowing* 3.61.

[17]*Cloud of Unknowing* 38.105.

[18]*Cloud of Unknowing* 3.62. Compare this with what Lewis says to "Malcolm" about his own attempt to use "wordless prayer": when he was a new Christian, he says, "I tried to pray without words at all—not to verbalise the mental acts. Even in praying for others I believe I tended to avoid their names and substituted mental images of them. I still think the prayer without words is the best—if one can really achieve it." *Letters to Malcolm: Chiefly on Prayer* (New York: Harvest Books, 1964), 11.

Pseudo-Dionysius the Areopagite, so-called because this sixth-century Platonic Byzantine theologian wrote under the pseudonym of Paul's disciple made on Mars Hill, as recorded in Acts 17:34. It was chiefly through Dionysius, Lewis explains, that so-called negative theology entered into the West; that is, an approach to theology that emphasizes by how far God eludes feeble human, rational powers: the incomprehensibility of God. In this way, Dionysius made up a kind of missing link between Plato, Plotinus, and the anonymous medieval English author of *The Cloud of Unknowing*.[19]

For the author of the *Cloud*, since God is beyond knowledge, you have to use love to overcome the gap,[20] but the great Dionysius takes a more cerebral approach: since God is the cause of being, he must be "above" being, and if he is above being, then there is no predicate (no attribute) that can be properly and fully applied to him. If the author of the *Cloud* is practical, warm, and impassioned, Dionysius is sublime, academic, brilliant, and challenging. He teaches an "apophatic theology," that is, a negative theology, in which we review traditional divine attributes—God's "names"—and declare them inadequate, or cancel them out, before we then super-affirm them as being true, but only in a transcendent way. In this way, we can avoid our tendency to forget the infinite distance between us and the Creator. Dionysius, in a stirring and impassioned passage that inspired the author of the *Cloud*, paints an image of the spiritual life as climbing up into higher, darker, and more remote regions of the spiritual life. The dwelling place of God is "on a plane above" speech and wisdom, and it "is made manifest only to those who travel through foul and fair, who pass beyond the summit of every holy ascent, who leave behind them every divine light, every voice, every word from heaven, and who plunge into the darkness where, as scripture proclaims, there dwells the One who is beyond all

---

[19]*DI*, 70.

[20]"All rational beings, angels and men, possess two faculties, the power of knowing and the power of loving. To the first, to the intellect, God who made them is forever unknowable, but to the second, to love, he is completely knowable, and that by every separate individual" (*Cloud of Unknowing* 4.63).

things."[21] But for Dionysius, this is just the first stage of detachment. There awaits an even bolder push out and up into God's darkness:

> But then he [Moses] breaks free of them, away from what sees and is seen, and he plunges into the truly mysterious darkness of un-knowing. Here, renouncing all that the mind may conceive, wrapped entirely in the intangible and the invisible, he belongs completely to him who is beyond everything. Here, being neither oneself nor someone else, one is supremely united by a completely unknowing inactivity of all knowledge, and knows beyond the mind by knowing nothing.[22]

This negative or apophatic theology—this keen sense of the "darkness of God"—was burned into the heart and imagination of C. S. Lewis through his reading of the old texts, but it was also reinforced for him by one of the very few modern theologians to make it onto the list with his beloved medieval writers: Rudolf Otto. At the beginning of the twentieth century, Otto wrote *The Idea of the Holy*, in which he pointed out that modern humanity has lost the sense of what the holy is. In contrast to modernity, which thinks of the apex of virtue as being nice, ancient languages and primitive religions treat holiness as that irrational overplus of meaning that extends beyond goodness. Holiness is a frightening and terrifying power that goes far beyond mere goodness. Otto coined the term *numinous* to capture this idea: "There is no religion in which [the numinous] does not live as the real innermost core, and without it no religion would be worthy of the name."[23] For Otto the numinous is that reality whose majesty is so far beyond our ordinary experience that it is difficult for us to classify it simply as good or bad: it is at once both alluring and dangerous, beautiful and terrifying. The numinous is mystery, which inspires a response of "stupor," "blank

---

[21]"The Mystical Theology," in *Pseudo-Dionysius: The Complete Works*, trans. Colum Luibheid, Classics of Western Spirituality (Mahwah, NJ: Paulist Press, 1987), 136.

[22]"Mystical Theology," 137.

[23]Rudolf Otto, *The Idea of the Holy*, trans. John Harvey (Oxford: Oxford University Press, 1958), 6.

wonder, an astonishment that strikes us dumb, amazement absolute."[24] It leaves the beholder in a state of trembling fear, religious dread, and awe. It is uncanny. It causes you to shudder, like the weird sisters in Macbeth, because it seems on a different plane of being. At the same time, Otto says it has an "urgent energy," as if it is on the verge of pouring forth, ever going out. Otto says that the mystics refer to this when they write about the "consuming fire" of God, "whose burning strength the mystic can hardly bear, but begs that the heat that has scorched him may be mitigated, lest he be himself destroyed by it."[25] At the very same time, Otto says, it is *mysterium fascinans*:

> It may appear to the mind an object of horror and dread, but at the same time it is no less something that allures with a potent charm, and the creature, who trembles before it, utterly cowed and cast down, has always at the same time the impulse to turn to it, may even to make it somehow his own. The "mystery" is for him not merely something to be wondered at but something that enters into him.[26]

All of these properties exist simultaneously in the numinous. It dwells on a different plane of reality, and for this reason it inspires *dread* in the creature who comes into contact with it. This is exactly what we find in the Old Testament, when Isaiah is given a vision of God, seated enthroned in his holiness (Is 6:1) or when Ezekiel is given an "appearance of the likeness of the glory of the LORD" (Ezek 1:28). These experiences shook the prophets to the core.

The concept of the numinous is absolutely everywhere in Lewis's writings. For instance, in *The Problem of Pain*, Lewis describes a special type of spiritual fear and dread. If we believed that there were a tiger in the next room, we would be afraid, but it would be a kind of biological fear of the senses.

---

[24]Otto, *Idea of the Holy*, 26.
[25]Otto, *Idea of the Holy*, 24.
[26]Otto, *Idea of the Holy*, 31.

But if you were told "There is a ghost in the next room," and believed it, you would feel, indeed, what is often called fear, but of a different kind. It would not be based on the knowledge of danger, for no one is primarily afraid of what a ghost may do to him, but of the mere fact that it is a ghost. It is "uncanny" rather than dangerous, and the special kind of fear it excites may be called Dread. With the Uncanny one has reached the fringes of the Numinous. Now suppose that you were told simply "There is a mighty spirit in the room," and believed it. Your feelings would then be even less like the mere fear of danger: but the disturbance would be profound. You would feel wonder and a certain shrinking—a sense of inadequacy to cope with such a visitant and of prostration before it.[27]

This idea of the numinous also reappears in fictional form. In his *Perelandra* of 1944 (published four years after *The Problem of Pain*), where Lewis looks "along the beam" at the numinous, describing the strange frisson that the narrator gets from accidentally coming into the presence of a superterrestrial creature, a bodiless, angelic being that speaks not through moving air but from intellect to intellect. The narrator writes that the creature seemed to have "reference to some horizontal, to some whole system of directions, based outside the Earth. . . . Its mere presence imposed that alien system on me and abolished the terrestrial horizon."[28] The narrator goes on,

I had no doubt at all that I was seeing an eldil, and little doubt that I was seeing the archon of Mars, the Oyarsa of Malacandra. And now that the thing had happened I was no longer in a condition of abject panic. My sensations were, it is true, in some ways very unpleasant. The fact that it was quite obviously not organic—the knowledge that the intelligence was somehow located in this homogenous cylinder of light but not related to it as our consciousness is related to our brains and nerves—was

---

[27]C. S. Lewis, *The Problem of Pain* (New York: Touchstone, 1996), 14-15.
[28]C. S. Lewis, *Perelandra: A Novel* (New York: Scribner, 2003), 17.

profoundly disturbing. It would not fit into our categories. The response which we ordinarily make to a living creature and that which we make to an inanimate object were here both equally inappropriate. . . . My fear was now of another kind. I felt sure that the creature was what we call "good," but I wasn't sure whether I liked "goodness" so much as I had supposed. . . . Here at last was a bit of that world from beyond the world, which I had always supposed that I loved and desired, breaking through and appearing to my senses: and I didn't like it, I wanted to go away.[29]

We can hear in this extraordinary passage all of the themes we have discussed: the sense of the distance between our world and the world beyond, the ontological terror it produces, as well as the shrinking feeling experienced by the merely mortal creature, who is overcome by a desire to hide. And yet despite the fact the narrator desires to be protected by every possible "distance, gulf, curtain, blanket, and barrier," he is still "drawn in."[30] It was also this encounter, this feeling of disorientation and falling, that Lewis associated with his own conversion, an encounter with "the naked Other, imageless (though our imagination salutes it with a hundred images), unknown, undefined, desired."[31]

Such authors represent the negative (or apophatic) tradition: bracing, icy, pure, clean, cold—like the thin air you breathe in the mountains during the winter. It's sobering, and purging. It wakes you up from that suffocating sentimentality that passes for religion, but which Lewis was absolutely allergic to. As salutary as such abrasive and astringent encounters with the "naked Other" can be, however, this awe, dread, and trembling does not amount to the Christian religion. To Lewis's mind, it did offer an attractive alternative, but it was missing a key element: what we could call the positive (or the

---

[29]Lewis, *Perelandra*, 17-18.
[30]Lewis, *Perelandra*, 18.
[31]*SBJ*, 221.

cataphatic). I will explore this positive element in the remainder of this
and in the next chapter.

CATAPHATIC THEOLOGY: THE PERSONAL WAY

In chapter eleven of *Miracles*, Lewis contrasts "Christianity" and mere
"religion." In words that recall his suspicion about his friend Bede
Griffiths's interest in Hinduism, he points out that the modern world
nods enthusiastically if we speak of God as an "indwelling principle"
or "great spiritual force pervading all things" or a "common mind." So
long as we remain vague and generic and impersonal, referring to the
highest being as if it were a "pool of generalized spirituality," we are
permitted to talk about religion; but "the temperature drops as soon
as you mention a God who has purposes and performs particular actions, who does one thing and not another, a concrete, choosing, com-
manding, prohibiting God with a determinate character. People
become embarrassed or angry."[32] Why? In part because thinking
about God as a concrete personality goes against the grain of our soft
evolutionary thinking about the "development" of human beings, according to which our image of God grows "less 'anthropomorphic'" as
we get "more enlightened."[33] But this would be a great mistake. The
reality is that when we qualify God's existence, saying with the mystics
"not thus,"[34] denying the adequacy of this or that particular human
attribute, we are doing so not because he is less human but because he
is "so brim-full of existence"[35] and because he is "plenitude of life and
energy and joy, therefore . . . [the mystics] have to pronounce that He
transcends those limitations."[36] The danger is to leave these negatives
unchecked by any positive intuition. The mystics talk of God as they
do, not because he is less human, but because he is supersaturated
being, more than human. Love must not be thought of as "something
less torrential or less sharp than our own temporary and derivative

[32]C. S. Lewis, *Miracles* (San Francisco: HarperSanFrancisco, 2001), 130.
[33]Lewis, *Miracles*, 130.
[34]Lewis, *Miracles*, 137.
[35]Lewis, *Miracles*, 141.
[36]Lewis, *Miracles*, 143.

passions."[37] It would be better to say he is transcorporeal and trans-personal, as opposed to incorporeal and impersonal:[38] "If we must have a mental picture to symbolize Spirit, we should represent it as something *heavier* than matter."[39] In sum, we have to correct our modern tendency to picture half consciously "a clear, still ocean, a dome of 'white radiance'" which smuggles in ideas of inertia or vacuity. It is true to say that in God there is no movement, but it would be better to say that God's motionlessness is his "infinite speed, which is the same thing as rest, but reached by a different . . . way of approach."[40] In language that echoes the mysterious scene of the *Voyage of the Dawn Treader*, Lewis says, "The stillness in which mysteries approach Him is intent and alert—at the opposite pole from sleep and reverie."[41] Lewis's description of Lucy and Caspian and Reepicheep's strange, quiet reverie, in which they hardly eat and hardly sleep, was his way of trying to correct the precarious tendencies of negative theology with a representation that makes it all feel like "something *heavier* than matter."[42]

But the very Platonic Christian spiritual tradition that offered the dramatic notions of negative theology also had resources for such a positive and concrete representation of God. In addition to the apophatic, there is another side to Dionysius and the tradition he inspired. In addition to such negative, apophatic language, he also uses statements of affirmation of, what he calls, the "supereminence" of God. Yes, God is inestimably higher than any worldly creature, and thus we have to practice "forgetfulness" or cancel out his names (negative or apophatic theology); it is also true that every creature, even if imperfectly, points or gestures toward that God who is above them. This is what is meant by positive or cataphatic theology. If a famous writer sends her daughter off to college, her professors might look for

---

[37]Lewis, *Miracles*, 148.
[38]Lewis, *Miracles*, 146.
[39]Lewis, *Miracles*, 147.
[40]Lewis, *Miracles*, 149.
[41]Lewis, *Miracles*, 149.
[42]Lewis, *Miracles*, 146.

traces of her mother's brilliance and literary proclivity, hints and gestures, even if, as an eighteen-year-old, her powers of expression are far from being developed. When I listen to one of Chopin's nocturnes, I get the feeling that I know something of the composer's soul, even if this piece was but a single day's composition. In this way, for Dionysius, although we must practice a negative theology, walking into the cloud of darkness to purify our imagination from believing that creatures adequately represent the supreme God, we also, on the flip side, *can* believe that creatures—rocks, light, angels, human beings—in their own limited way can stutter and mumble something about God to us. This is the positive approach, in which creatures, analogically, point toward God.

There is, clearly, a tension between these positive and negative tendencies, and, in light of that tension, we can appreciate why Lewis held a third medieval mystic—Nicholas of Cusa (also known as Cusanus)—in such high regard. Nicholas of Cusa, a German-Italian cardinal and mystical author from the fifteenth century, has been called the last of the medievals, or the first of the moderns (a kind of bookend figure to the medieval period, with Boethius on the other side, who is sometimes called the last of the Romans and the first of the medievals). Cusanus, like Lewis after him, was fascinated by the dramatic juxtaposition of God's transcendence and God's proximity. For Cusanus, God is what he calls the "maximum," that "beyond which there can be nothing greater."[43] But, Cusanus explains in his characteristically dense and enigmatic way, we can find these maxima in innumerable places, such as the infinitely small, because they too are "maximally minimal," and thus have something in common with the "maximally" infinite. On the cusps of the Scientific Revolution, Cusanus often resorts to mathematics to illustrate his points. For example, he argues, if the diameter of the circle were stretched, the circle would turn into an ellipse, and the curve of the circle would be

---

[43]Nicholas of Cusa, *On Learned Ignorance,* as found in, *Selected Spiritual Writings,* ed. and trans. H. Lawrence Bond, Classics of Western Spirituality (New York: Paulist Press, 1997), 1.2, 89.

flattened out somewhat. But if the diameter were stretched infinitely, the curve of the ellipse would fold up into a line, and thus a line can be said to contain within itself the circle.[44] By a similarly strange argument, a kind of medieval anticipation of the discovery of calculus, Cusanus imagines that triangles are also present in lines of infinite length. And so, within this geometrical figure of absolute simplicity (the line) but also of incomprehensible length, we have, pulsing, all manner of geometrical shapes folded up within it, analogously to the Hawking Radiation put off by a black hole, which contains within it everything that has ever come into its gravitation field. All of this helps us understand what Cusanus means by calling the world a "contracted maximum." The universe is an infinite set of micro-infinities. Or, in the peculiar style of Cusanus,

> The infinite form is received only in a finite way; consequently, every creature is, as it were, a finite infinity or a created god, so that it exists in the way in which this could best be. It is as if the Creator had spoken: "Let it be made," and because God, who is eternity itself, could not be made, that was made which could be made, which would be as much like God as possible.[45]

In other words, Cusanus imagines an ebullient, generous God, who, though desirous of sharing as much of himself as possible, can only donate as much of himself as the creature is capable of receiving. And yet, God is always eager to share more, to draw closer to his creatures, to saturate them to the extent they can admit him, so that they too can be "brim-full of existence." This is what Cusanus calls the "coincidence of opposites," the reconciliation of seemingly opposing things: in this case, God's immanence and transcendence. Or as Lewis puts it in *Miracles*, echoing Cusanus's *On Learned Ignorance*, "God is present in a great many different modes: not present in matter as He is present in man, not present in all men as in some, not present in any other man as in Jesus."[46]

---

[44]Nicholas of Cusa, *On Learned Ignorance* 1.13.

[45]Nicholas of Cusa, *On Learned Ignorance* 2.2, 134.

[46]Lewis, *Miracles*, 137.

When we call Lewis a mystic, then, we have to remember that he, like Cusanus, was intent on practicing this very medieval "coincidence of opposites," or what we might call a double focus—the simultaneous reality of God's infinite "transcendence" and of his radical presence. At the same moment, God is infinitely remote in his majesty—the numinous, the awe-ful, even the "terrible"—but also closer to me than I am to myself. God at once is, in an awesome phrase quoted in *Letters to Malcolm*, the glory, the "light from behind the sun,"[47] but also the one who knocks quietly on the door of my heart (as Lewis recalled in his own conversion narrative), moved by such a love as to wish to be as near me as possible, to the extent that my matter can admit his presence. The medieval scholar sums up the necessity of such bifocal vision in *Letters to Malcolm*:

> I fully agree that the relationship between God and a man is more private and intimate than any possible relationship between two fellow creatures. Yes, but at the same time, in another way, a greater distance between the participants. We are approaching—well I won't say "the Wholly Other," for I suspect that is meaningless, but the Unimaginably and Insupportably Other. We ought to be—sometimes I hope one is—simultaneously aware of closest proximity and infinite distance.[48]

This bifocal vision of mysticism—this simultaneous awareness—also makes its appearance in Lewis's fiction, illustrated particularly brilliantly in Lucy's encounter with Aslan in *Prince Caspian*, which I will describe to conclude this chapter.

Lucy, the Mystic

After a long day of toilsome travel, the whole company, made up of Lucy, Peter, Edmund, and a dwarf, stops to rest. All drift off to sleep quickly, except Lucy. Earlier that day, Lucy had thought she had seen Aslan, even if none of the others could confirm her suspicion. And so,

---

47Lewis, *Letters to Malcolm*, 28.
48Lewis, *Letters to Malcolm*, 13.

excited, she lies there, "alert": "Instead of getting drowsier she was getting more awake—with an odd night-time, dreamish kind of wakefulness."[49] It soon becomes clear that Lucy is animated by the same vigilance Lewis attributes to the mystic in *Miracles*, and soon we hear not only about Lucy's wakefulness, but also of an abundance of excessive light. The whole world starts to grow transparent, letting in a light from some mysterious, deeper source: "The Creek was growing brighter. She knew now that the moon was on it, though she couldn't see the moon. And now she began to feel that the whole forest was coming awake like herself. . . . 'This is lovely,' said Lucy to herself. It was cool and fresh; delicious smells were floating everywhere."[50] What is more, Lucy feels that the trees are on the verge of waking up, just on the brink of speaking, but then the whole scene dies away in a disappointing anticlimax.

But this disappointment, of the world falling back into mute unconsciousness, is not to last for long. Indeed, things are just about to go wild. In the first scene of Lucy's wakefulness, we had an eerie and spooky moonlight, with wind in the trees, a kind of pure paganism. But on the second night, we have all of that with one important difference: Aslan will be present, and not just present, but playfully and gleefully and (almost) childishly present. The numinous is now also immanent. On the second night, Lucy hears a voice calling her by name, and although it is night "the whole forest landscape around her was almost as clear as day, though it looked wilder."[51] Soon she discovers that all the trees are moving, dancing to a tune she could not hear. Wildness is blended with the solemnity of the night:

> She knew she herself was wide awake, wider than anyone usually is. She went fearlessly in among [the trees], dancing herself as she leaped this way and that to avoid being run into by these huge partners. But she was only half interested in them. She wanted to get beyond them to something else; it was from

---

[49]C. S. Lewis, *Prince Caspian* (New York: HarperCollins, 1984), 88.
[50]Lewis, *Prince Caspian*, 88.
[51]Lewis, *Prince Caspian*, 103.

beyond them that the dear voice had called. . . . And then—oh joy! For he was there: the huge Lion, shining white in the moon-light, with his huge black shadow underneath him. . . . She felt her heart would burst if she lost a moment. And the next thing she knew was that she was kissing him and putting her arms as far round his neck as she could and burying her face in the beau-tiful rich silkiness of his mane. "Aslan, Aslan. Dear Aslan," sobbed Lucy. "At last." The great beast rolled over on his side so that Lucy fell, half sitting and half lying between his front paws. He bent forward and just touched her nose with his tongue. His warm breath came all round her. She gazed up into the large wise face. "Welcome, child," he said.[52]

In the midst of the eerie and numinous landscape, Lucy's encounter with Aslan is intimately childlike, as the lion, rolling around, licks her. But soon Aslan will go on to pose questions to her, gently letting her own conscience speak. In this exchange, Lucy will admit her own lack of faithfulness, her fear that others would think she was just a silly little girl, fear that her beloved siblings won't see him on the next day's march, fear that she will be alone. Aslan concludes their conversation, "But come. We have no time to lose." In other words, in this scene, perhaps more completely than any other in Lewis's imaginative writings, we find the medievalist bringing together all the varied me-lodic strands of his thoughts on mysticism. It is a blend of the terrible, the awful, the profound, and the transcendent; but also the unexpectedly down-to-earth, the homely, the personal, the lovingly intimate. But in the end, it is not to last for long. Such mystical en-counters are sweet but brief. Every Sunday turns back into a Monday morning, but they do help us to rearm our will with the desire to attend to those daily acts of faithful obedience.

---

[52]Lewis, *Prince Caspian*, 107.

CHAPTER SEVEN

DEEP CONVERSION
and UNVEILING

When the "It" Becomes a "You"

*People who are naturally religious find difficulty in understanding
the horror of such a revelation. . . . Remember, I had always
wanted, above all things, not to be "interfered with." I
had wanted (mad wish) "to call my soul my own."*

C. S. LEWIS, *SURPRISED BY JOY*

THROUGHOUT THIS BOOK, we've seen how the man who referred
to himself as "the last dinosaur" felt a closer kinship with the old
writers than he did with those philosophers and theologians of his
own age. Throughout his personal letters, his assessments of Ki-
erkegaard, Maritain, Tillich, Sartre, and Barth remained tepid. In a
blunt assessment for Corbin Scott Carnell, he reported,

> As for moderns, Tillich and Brunner I don't know at all. Maritain
> I tried but did not admire. He seems to say in 10 pages of polysyl-
> labic abstraction what Scripture or the old writers wd. say in a
> couple of sentences. Kierkegaard still means almost nothing to
> me. I read one book of Niebuhr's—I can't remember the

title—and, on the whole, reacted against it. I tried Berdyaev, but
he seemed to me terribly repetitive; one paragraph wd. do for
what he spins out into a book.[1]

And Sartre? His thought was just a recycling of idealism ("Berkeleyan
metaphysic") now "in the mind of an atheist with a bad liver!"[2] And
although his French prose had "a sort of wintry grandeur," Lewis just
"couldn't see that he was a real philosopher."[3] Barth? "Barth I have
never read, or not that I remember."[4] His attitude toward modern
philosophers and theologians was humorously indifferent.

There was one exception though: the Jewish philosopher Martin
Buber, whom Lewis read not long after the publication of the English
translation of *I and Thou* in 1937, even if on the first reading he had a
massive allergic reaction. For a long while he was unable to formulate
precisely his own thoughts on the book, but also unable to ignore it.
On August 1, 1942, he ordered Owen Barfield, "Read Athanasius *De
Incarnatione* . . . and also tell me what to think about Martin Buber. *I
and Thou* (publishers T & T Clark). I think it is rather rot but am not
sure."[5] Around the same time (July 29, 1942) he earnestly asked Sister
Penelope, "Have you read Martin Buber's *I and Thou*. Tell me what I
am to think of it? From Heaven, or (very subtly) from Hell? I'm by no
means sure."[6] But over the next two decades his assessment of the
Jewish philosopher mellowed. By 1955, he could admit a qualified admiration for Buber: "I thought Buber had grasped one most important
truth: the immense depth of the Thou experience (firstly, of God, and
secondly, of my neighbour) and the danger of letting it get submerged
by the shallower He or, still shallower, Thou experience."[7] By the 1960s
even his qualifications had begun to fade away. He had come to realize
that Buber was, after all, from heaven: "We cry 'Father.' . . . As Buber

---

[1]*Letters*, 3:978-79.
[2]*Letters*, 3:24.
[3]*Letters*, 3:1238.
[4]*Letters*, 3:980.
[5]*Letters*, 2:528.
[6]*Letters*, 2:522.
[7]*Letters*, 3:631.

might say God is most fully real to us as Thou, less so as He, least so as It. We must worship the Thou, not the He in our own minds, which is just as much an image (therefore a possible idol) as a figure of wood or stone."[8] And so we are not too surprised that by the 1963 *Letters to Malcolm*, we have this glowing summation of Buber's thought:

> He reveals Himself as Person: or reveals that in Him which is Person. For—dare one say it? in a book it would need pages of qualification and insurance—God is in some measure to a man as that man is to God. The door in God that opens is the door he knocks at. . . . The Person in Him—He is more than a person— meets those who can welcome or at least face it. He speaks as "I" when we truly call Him "Thou." (How good Buber is!).[9]

We are on sacred ground for Lewis.

Ordinarily, in our scientific and technological age, we think of things [and now people, too!] as "facts": atoms obediently moving by laws of motion and changing according to chemical laws of inter-action. But Buber was interested in that quality of experience—the "you" (or, to use the older intimate form, the "thou")—in which I am overwhelmed by an experience of a person, a relationship, an en-counter for which no set of facts seems adequate to explain. Lewis found this a healthy corrective to the perennial tendency in "religion" to reduce an I-Thou encounter with God into an I-It affair of the head. In Lewis's eyes, modern spirituality was only the latest revival of a very ancient "pantheism" according to which a cerebral "principle" or "life force" pervades the world. While such a "life force" might solicit our hushed admiration and inspire our reverence, it does not irrupt into our world as a person. But Christians, unlike the noble pagans, have the awful privilege of assenting with a "will to be known" and to let ourselves be treated "in relation to God, not as things but as persons." In a world we can "unveil" before God.[10]

---

[8]*Letters*, 3:1173.

[9]C. S. Lewis, *Letters to Malcolm: Chiefly on Prayer* (New York: Harvest Books, 1964), 21.

[10]Lewis, *Letters to Malcolm*, 21.

These related ideas—the I-Thou encounter with God and the difficulty of letting myself unveil before him—was for Lewis the great (and
unexpected) discovery of history, the insight that all previous religious
and philosophical efforts had been oriented toward but had not known.
It was also the crowning moment of his own conversion. As one should
expect now in this book, Lewis was indebted to the medieval world for
phrases and terms to articulate even something as personal as his
conversion story.

Praeparatio Evangelica: Waiting for the Thou

The medieval world widely held a philosophy of history that was
summed up by the phrase *praeparatio evangelica*, by which they meant
that the natural movements of non-Christian cultures, even if without
cognizant cooperation, played a crucial role in preparing the world for
the gospel of Christ. Egypt falls to Nineveh; Nineveh is captured by
Babylon. Persia conquers Babylon, before being conquered by the
Greek Alexander, whose empire was then handed over to the Romans.
And when the world was made ready—with roads and commerce and
magistrates and laws—Christ came into the world.

This sort of sentiment—of benighted people accidentally groping
their way through history toward Christ—can be found in Dante's
characterization of the Roman poet Statius, the author of the *Thebaid*:
a massive, mannerist, epic poem treating the battle fought among Oe-
dipus's sons for Thebes after their father's death, beloved in the Middle
Ages and neglected among moderns (unduly, Lewis thought). Although there is no historical evidence to suggest that Statius
(AD 45–96) was a Christian, Dante, employing his poetic license, invented a backstory, like some writer of fan lit after the author's death.
In Dante's version, Statius, now in the afterlife, tells the story of his
alleged secret conversion to Christianity, which came about, strangely
enough, by reading the pagan Virgil!

> It was you who first
> Set me toward Parnassus to drink in its grottoes,
> And you who first lit my way toward God.

You were as one who goes by night, carrying
The light behind him—it is no help to him,
But instructs all those who follow—

When you said: "The centuries turn new again.
Just returns with the first age of man,
And new progeny descends from heaven."

Through you I was a poet, through you a Christian.[11]

The poem to which Statius alludes ("when you said . . .") comes from a set of minor poems by Virgil, called the *Eclogues*, a series of bucolic poems about the peaceful lives of shepherds who dreamily walk about all day in the Mediterranean countryside thinking about love and drowsily singing poetry for their lovers while reclining in the shade of plane trees. But the fourth of these poems has a different tone. In *that* poem, Virgil briefly sets aside "humble" matters to make bold, world-historical predictions, cryptically hinting at some hoped-for Roman savior who would end the brutal period of civil wars that were shredding Virgil's Italy. This is the famous "Fourth Eclogue," which was read by medieval Christians as a messianic prophecy:

Now the last age by Cumae's Sibyl sung
Has come and gone, and the majestic roll
Of circling centuries begins anew:
Justice returns, returns old Saturn's reign,
With a new breed of men sent down from heaven.
Only do thou, at the boy's birth in whom
The iron shall cease, the golden race arise,
. . . For thee, O boy,
. . . locks afield
Shall of the monstrous lion have no fear.
. . . The serpent too shall die,
Die shall the treacherous poison-plant.[12]

---

[11]Dante, *Purgatorio* 22.64-73. This and the following references to *Purgatorio* are my translation.

[12]Virgil, "Fourth Eclogue," trans. John Dryden, http://classics.mit.edu/Virgil/eclogue.4.iv.html.

Virgil, of course, intended the poem as an expression of hope for an end to the civil conflict of his day, but his use of imagery, which inexplicably echoes the biblical promises of the prophet Isaiah, thrilled medieval readers. They thought they had found a noble pagan who, in a moment of pious reflection, was overshadowed by the Holy Spirit and became a vessel for the utterance of salvific promises that he himself could barely understand. Virgil, they breathlessly felt, was on the threshold of Christianity: predicting a new golden age, an end to war, an age of plenty and fecundity, an epoch in which the lion will lie down with the lamb. One of this poem's first accidental converts, according to Dante's medieval imagination, was Statius.

As skeptical, modern scholars, we can only smile condescendingly at such quaint medieval readings of the past, but such medieval commonplaces, irritants for modern readers, became personal, scholarly challenges to C. S. Lewis, who loved to take up and defend the most recalcitrant of old beliefs, especially when they had been obvious to everyone in the premodern world and have only become dubious to us. As a scholar, Lewis devoted his earliest book to the strange literary phenomena of courtly love and allegory (*Allegory of Love*), putting them on trial, as it were, to see what enduring values lay hidden under the historical peculiarities of that bizarre poetic form and exotic courtly ritual. And so, consistent with this habit of rehabilitating old ideas, Lewis wrote an essay trying to discover the reasons that might have induced the Italian poet to include Statius as a Christian in his imaginative afterlife. Lewis argues that in Statius's poetry we find numerous Christian doctrines anticipated: conviction of sin, love of piety, natural morality, and a belief in a loving, theistic fatherly providence. All of this made him an ideal candidate to serve in Dante's imagination as a forerunner of Christianity, a pagan who, like Virgil, had come to the threshold of Christianity by following on those noble natural impulses. As we will see, Statius looks a lot like pre-Christian Lewis: a man of high sensibility and virtuous inclinations, a reverent follower of the "Tao," pious worshiper of the "unknown God," until the fateful moment when that divine, impersonal life force revealed himself, as a person.[13]

When we keep in mind the medieval understanding of *praeparatio evangelica* as found in Dante and other medieval authors, then we have eyes to see the role it played in Lewis's own assessment of history. Indeed, the idea of *praeparatio evangelica* is not just at the heart of Lewis's own conversion but also at the heart of Lewis's "philosophy of religion." In broad terms, Lewis thought that if Christianity were true then primitive religious ritual, mythological tales, and even world religions "may well be a *preparatio evangelica*, divine hinting in poetic and ritual form at the same central truth which was later focused and (so to speak) historicized in the Incarnation."[14] Lewis described himself as one who "first approached Christianity from a delighted interest in, and reverence for, the best pagan imagination, who loved Balder before Christ and Plato before St. Augustine," and so it was important for him to be able to explain what was true about non-Christian religions. For Lewis, it was *not* the case that "999 were pure nonsense and the thousandth (fortunately) true. My conversion, very largely, depended on recognizing Christianity as the completion, the actualization, the entelechy, of something that had never been wholly absent from the mind of man."[15] Christianity is the prince of myths, the ultimate and final myth, what our scholar of medieval literature called a "true myth." By this he meant that Christianity was a mythological picture of the world with one important and extraordinary difference: its mythological features entered into history and time and wore a face. Christianity is the pure white light that had revealed itself in a myriad of fragmented colors, as refracted through the prism of history over centuries before the advent of Christ. Indeed, for Lewis, all humanity has enjoyed some portion of this

---

[13]"Dante's Statius," in *Studies in Medieval and Renaissance Literature*, Canto Classics (Cambridge: Cambridge University Press, 1998), 94-102.
[14]"Religion Without Dogma?," *EC*, 166.
[15]"Religion Without Dogma?," *EC*, 166.

divine light, even if Christianity (and Judaism) have had privileged access to it:

> The Divine Light, we are told, "lighteneth every man." We should, therefore, expect to find in the imagination of great Pagan teachers and myth-makers some glimpse of that theme which we believe to be the very plot of the whole cosmic story—the theme of incarnation, death and rebirth. And the differences between the Pagan Christs (Balder, Osiris, etc) and the Christ Himself is much what we should expect to find. The Pagan stories are all about someone dying and rising, either every year, or else nobody knows where and nobody knows when. The Christian story is about a historical personage, whose execution can be dated pretty accurately, under a named Roman magistrate. . . . It is not the difference between falsehood and truth. It is the difference between a real event on the one hand and dim dreams or premonitions of that same event on the other. It is like watching something come gradually into focus: first it hangs in the clouds of myth and ritual, vast and vague, then it condenses, grows hard and in a sense small, as a historical event in the first-century Palestine.[16]

"God became man" is tantamount to saying, "myth became fact." Christianity is the culmination of the mythological age, while at the same time the "final" myth, given that it "condenses" legendary longing into a concrete, historical, flesh-bound person, a story that is then entrusted to the historical succession of people who make up the church. Myth became a person. The It becomes a You.

FROM MYTH TO PERSON: LEWIS'S CONVERSION

What is extraordinary, though, is that the medieval scholar read the very processes of *praeparatio evangelica*, which had operated at the macrolevel of history, as also playing out at the more personal level of psychology. In his youth, he had been haunted by vague longings,

---

[16]"Is Theology Poetry?," *EC*, 16.

ambiguous premonitions, moments of inner aching and longing, which he later described in rich detail as the sort of strange, icy sensation filled with an "unendurable sense of desire and loss."[17] He called it by various names, "Joy," or "pure 'Northernness,'" a vision of "huge, clear spaces hanging above the Atlantic in the endless twilight of Northern summer, remoteness, severity."[18] But to his surprise, as he continued to read, he found something like this haunting quality of religion in Christian authors too. He began to feel like he was being hunted and surrounded. A whole host was after him and against him, beloved authors, beloved friends, new acquaintances, and students: "Nearly everyone was now (one way or another) in the pack; Plato, Dante, MacDonald, Herbert, Barfield, Tolkien, Dyson, Joy itself. Everyone and everything had joined the other side. Even my own pupil Griffiths . . . though not yet a believer himself, did his share."[19] The preconversion Lewis was in the same position as Virgil or Statius.

And yet, enjoying myth and being a Christian are not the same thing. It took a dinner party with two Christians, Hugo Dyson and J. R. R. Tolkien, for Lewis to come to believe that the peculiar nature of *Christian* mythology lay in its historical, personal reality. As is well known, the three men went for a walk through the grounds of Lewis's college, Magdalen, and discussed mythology, metaphor, and Christianity. Lewis was still having difficulty believing that "Christian mythology" could be more than just an inspiring bit of literature, for, after all, although mythological tales are beautiful and moving, they are, in the end, "lies and therefore worthless, even though breathed through silver."[20] But Tolkien disagreed. Here is Humphrey Carpenter's classic retelling of the scene:

> "No," said Tolkien, "They are not lies."

[17]*SBJ*, 73.

[18]*SBJ*, 73.

[19]*SBJ*, 225.

[20]Humphrey Carpenter, *The Inklings: C. S. Lewis, J. R. R. Tolkien, Charles Williams, and Their Friends* (London: HarperCollins, 1978), 43.

Just then (Lewis afterwards recalled) there was a "rush of wind which came so suddenly on the still, warm evening and sent so many leaves pattering down that we thought it was raining. We held our breath."

When Tolkien resumed, he took his arguments from the very thing that they were watching.

"You look at trees, he said, and call them 'trees,' and probably you do not think twice about the word. You call a star a 'star,' and think nothing more of it. But you must remember that these words, 'tree,' 'star' were (in their original forms) names given to these objects by people with very different views than yours. To you, a tree is simply a vegetable organism, a star simply a ball of inanimate matter moving along a mathematical course. But the first men to talk of 'trees' and 'stars' saw things very differently. To them, the world was alive with mythological beings. They saw these stars as living silver, bursting into flame in answer to the eternal music. They saw the sky as a jewelled tent, and the earth as the womb whence all living things have come. To them, the whole creation was 'myth-woven and elf-patterned.'"[21]

In other words, the very names from a different age have lingered and survived into our world, carrying with them a faint perfume from distant times. We cannot even speak without, however obliquely, thinking in myth. Moreover, the myths weren't essentially untrue. They were based on deep ancient intuitions—the premonitions of the *praeparatio evangelica*—that the physical world was moving "in answer to the eternal music," based on the fundamental belief that God uses the natural world to express "himself through the minds of poets, and [uses] images in their 'mythopoeia' to express fragments of his eternal truth."[22]

There was, of course, one final step: to encounter God not as a force or idea (or impersonal It), but as a person. Throughout the last of his

---

[21]Carpenter, *Inklings*, 43.
[22]Carpenter, *Inklings*, 44.

pagan years, Lewis began to feel like he was trying to block something out, and that he had the power to open a door, and let it all come in if he so chose. From the perspective of the beleaguered atheist, what was worse was that this abstract spirit that Lewis acknowledged with a vague principle of allegiance had begun to feel personal, the traditional God of religion. Lewis began to feel that this person, not just a principle, was personally asking for the door to open, and he "would not argue about it. He only said, 'I am the Lord'; 'I am that I am'; 'I am.'"[23] Lewis began to feel almost afraid, but at the same time curious and desirous of opening the door.[24] Shortly after this sense of a personal call, he finally gave in: "In the Trinity Term of 1929 I gave in, and admitted that God was God, and knelt and prayed: perhaps, that night, the most dejected and reluctant convert in all England."[25]

I have repeated details my readers will be familiar with in order to draw out a significant parallel. Lewis's own description of his conversion, according to which an unknown urge—a desire for "Joy"— tugging, anonymously and namelessly within, turned out to be a loving person. This is an autobiographical recapitulation of what he believed had taken place on the general level of human history. In other words, Lewis's own conversion is a microcosmic reflection of the slow historical preparation of the human race, the *praeparatio evangelica*. Over the course of centuries, an indefinable and indefatigable longing found its expression first in myths, legends, and religious rituals, but eventually "condensed" into the historical person Jesus Christ, analogously to how young Jack's reading and aesthetic experiences were preparation for encountering Christ. In his very conversion story, we have a reflection of his philosophy of world religion, as well as his philosophy of history. But for Lewis the story does not end at

---

[23]*SBJ*, 227.
[24]"I became aware that I was holding something at bay, or shutting something out. . . . I felt myself being, there and then, given a free choice. I could open the door or keep it shut. . . . Neither choice was presented as a duty; no threat or promise was attached to either, though I knew that to open the door . . . meant the incalculable. The choice appeared to be momentous but it was also strangely unemotional. I chose to open" (*SBJ*, 224).
[25]*SBJ*, 228-29.

conversion. There remains a process that is peculiarly difficult in modernity, a process I will call "deep conversion" or "unveiling."

DEEP CONVERSION AND UNVEILING

According to Charles Taylor, one of the effects of the radical cultural shift that occurred between AD 1500 and 2000 is that we moderns "conceive of ourselves as having inner depths. We might even say that the depths which were previously located in the cosmos, the enchanted world, are now more readily placed within."[26] In other words, the "disenchantment" of the cosmos was accompanied by a psychological effect, one that, as we have seen, Lewis was attentive to his whole life: the modern tendency to possess a cranky irritability about our own private, inner space. Lewis thought that in modernity human beings have a particular tendency to think of what is inside them—thoughts, dreams, feelings, emotions, desires—as a kind of inner sanctum, which they might sometimes share but is where they feel most real and authentic. Lewis thought this tendency to psychological individualism was not only peculiarly modern but presented a special obstacle to loving God, given that we are constitutionally reluctant to admit God into the inner chamber of our life, even when we are committed to living externally in a moral way. We draw a line, and want to keep our own as our own. In a fascinating essay, "A Slip of the Tongue," Lewis sums up this reluctance to deep conversion:

> I say my prayers, I read a book of devotion, I prepare for, or receive, the Sacrament. But while I do these things, there is, so to speak, a voice inside me that urges caution. It tells me to be careful, to keep my head, not to go too far, not to burn my boats. I come into the presence of God with a great fear, lest anything should happen to me within that presence which will prove too intolerably inconvenient when I have to come out again into my "ordinary" life. I don't want to be carried away into any resolution which I shall afterwards regret. . . .

---

[26]Charles Taylor, *A Secular Age* (Cambridge, MA: Belknap, 2007), 540.

> This is my endlessly recurrent temptation: to go down to that
> Sea (I think St. John of the Cross called God a sea) and there
> neither dive nor swim nor float, but only dabble and splash,
> careful not to get out of my depth and holding on to the lifeline
> which connects me with my things temporal.[27]

Lewis's words give a sense of the onerousness, even the fear, of "unveiling" completely. For a modern soul, even for a Christian, this
final sense of "privacy," this lingering desire to hold on to that which
is "my own" is potentially dangerous. Even when we are not talking
about sinful things per se, but benign and simple pleasures, like a
"mother's love" and the "basket with its warm, animal smell," as Lewis
put it in *The Four Loves*, or walks to enjoy a landscape, or looking up
old words, or (as in *The Screwtape Letters*) a cup of hot chocolate,
there can be a fatal possessiveness, to have them as our own and in
perpetuity, to hold them with the fear of losing them, not to take
them as gifts, to treasure them just because they are no one else's.
Those simple loves are perilous if they create within us a small reservation whose boundaries we jealously patrol to keep from God. And
although these loves in and of themselves can be benign, they silently
lodge themselves within us, create barriers and walls, and make it
difficult—perhaps even impossible—to fully choose God, or to let
ourselves be viewed by God. Lewis exquisitely called this angry and
territorial voice that was resistant to conversion the desire to be free
from "interference":

> No word in my vocabulary expressed deeper hatred than the
> word *Interference*. But Christianity placed at the center what
> then seemed to me a transcendental Interferer. If its picture
> were true then no sort of "treaty with reality" could ever be
> possible. There was no region even in the innermost depth of
> one's soul (nay, there least of all) which one could surround
> with a barbed wire fence and guard with a notice No

---

[27]C. S. Lewis, "A Slip of the Tongue," in *The Weight of Glory: And Other Addresses* (New York: HarperOne, 1980), 185-87.

Admittance. And that was what I wanted; some area, however small, of which I could say to all other beings, "This is my business and mine only."[28]

To let myself be unveiled, and to let God enter into even these small and humble things, can be seen as the perfection of that process of conversion, the perfection of that process from the impersonal to the personal. It is the culmination of letting ourselves become persons before God.

THE THICKENING-UP PROCESS

There is, then, a strange drama within. On the one hand, we are naturally geared toward bliss, and as such we are naturally inclined to God. We carry around within us an "inner wound" that expresses itself in a longing to dwell in the fullness of his presence, as well as a restless dissatisfaction with anything but that. At the same time, though, we are afraid of letting God move into the inner sanctuary of the heart. We don't want to admit him into the very center of our personality. We don't want to give up the fatal privacy of our dreams, ambitions, goals, hopes, and, sometimes, resentments, because we don't want to die to what seems to be our truest self. We would rather cling to these small things, holding them before us like a veil to shield our face from God. Thus, in an Augustinian key, Lewis establishes a kind of general law: what is truest about us, our best self, is within and it is spiritual, but we are continually attracted to the low-hanging, half-rotten, overripe fruit on the periphery of our being: "All the time You were more inward than the most inward place of my heart and loftier than the highest."[29] What strikes us as most real is that which is tangible, visible, external, and physical, and thus we spend our life in exile, as it were, from ourselves, seeking meaning outside of our truest self. Indeed, we make these external goods—which are transitory and imperfect—a part of our identity, such that we have a difficult time conceiving of ourselves apart from them.[30]

---

[28]*SBJ*, 172.
[29]Augustine, *Confessions*, trans. F. J. Sheed, 2nd ed. (Indianapolis: Hackett, 2006), 44.
[30]Augustine, *Confessions*, 27.

In a particularly difficult passage of *The Great Divorce*, a mother who spent her days mourning for a beloved son who died in his youth meets her brother in heaven. She is disappointed to meet Reginald, because she had hoped rather to be greeted by her son, Michael. Reginald replies that she *will* get to see Michael, but she will need to become a denser, realer person first. "How?" the mother asks.

> "I'm afraid the first step is a hard one. . . . You will become solid enough for Michael to perceive you when you learn to want someone else besides Michael. I don't say 'more than Michael,' not as a beginning. That will come later. It's only a little germ of a desire for God that we need to start the process."
>
> Pam replies: "Oh, you mean religion and all that sort of thing? This is the hardly the moment. . . ."

Her brother replies,

> "But, Pam, do think! Don't you see you are not beginning at all as long as you are in that state of mind? You're treating God only as a means to Michael. But the whole thickening treatment consists in learning to want God for his own sake."[31]

In light of what we have seen in this chapter, the drama of the scene is found in Pam's difficulty in admitting God into the inner sanctum of her love.

Although Lewis never backed away from this extraordinary call to "unveiling," he also thought that such a level of self-revelation was not something we could well achieve on our own. But "I am not in despair," he adds reassuringly in "A Slip of the Tongue," after confessing to loving creaturely goods with too much zeal: "At this point I become what some would call very Evangelical. I do not think any efforts of my own will can end once and for all this craving for limited liabilities, this fatal reservation. Only God can."[32] It is this extraordinary effort by God—as the judge of the secret things of the heart—which can be found in the

---

[31]C. S. Lewis, *The Great Divorce* (New York: Macmillan, 1978), 92.
[32]Lewis, "A Slip of the Tongue," 191.

judgment scene in *Till We Have Faces*, in which Lewis portrays all of these themes woven together: an I-Thou encounter in which Orual must, quite literally, "unveil." As we will see, this was Lewis's attempt to rewrite a scene from medieval literature that had burned itself on his imagination: Dante's encounter with Beatrice in the Earthly Garden. Indeed, we know that Lewis loved the final canti of *Purgatorio* in particular. They were, he confessed in a letter, not only the literary model for his own "Tragedian" scene in *The Great Divorce* but indeed the very kernel for *The Great Divorce* itself, around which everything else grew up.[33] Lewis wrote the scene with the Tragedian, who cannot make a deep confession, as a way of exploring what would have happened if Dante had failed at his own confession before Beatrice. For that reason, I'll turn to that scene as Lewis's gold standard for a deep conversion, before concluding with Lewis's own attempt to "rip away the veil and reveal the first and eternal things" in the final scene *Till We Have Faces*.[34]

DANTE, ORUAL, AND UNVEILING

For the first-time reader of Dante, it seems that the journey has almost come to a conclusion by the time the pilgrim reaches the end of *Purgatorio*. Even Dante's guide Virgil seems to think so, instructing Dante,

> you may sit down or move among these
> until the fair eyes come, rejoicing.[35]

At any moment, then, the long-awaited meeting between lover and beloved will take place. But instead of the hoped-for romantic reunion in a field with long grasses, everything spins terribly out of control. A supernatural apocalyptic procession alights within the garden, to the pilgrim's complete awe and bemusement:

> And behold, a shining suddenly ran through
> the great forest on all sides, such that it made
> me wonder if it were lightning.

---

[33]See January 22, 1946, *Letters*, 2:699-700; March 28, 1953, *Letters*, 3:313-14.
[34]Markos, *From Plato to Christ*, 207.
[35]Dante, *Purgatorio* 27.133-34.

> But since lightning, as soon as it comes,
> ceases, and this, lasting, shone brighter and
> brighter, in my thought I said: "What thing is this?"[36]

The pilgrim has difficulty even identifying the nature of the eerie event. The images he uses to describe it become more unnatural as the canto proceeds. The company attending Beatrice flames more brightly than the moon at midnight,[37] and as they advance the air is left colored,[38] as if they were so steeped in heavenly light that they burn color into the air as they pass through it. The poet turns to this synesthetic blending of images to gesture at what he saw, as if wildly gesticulating at something well beyond language (he sees sounds and hears sights). The world of nature begins to melt down in the heat of this extraordinary event.[39]

But from there it only gets worse. From the midst of this huge procession steps out Beatrice, Dante's long-lost love. But she is now veiled from Dante's eyes.[40] In a confusion of emotion, Dante turns toward his first guide, Virgil, but who without announcement had silently left. The pilgrim turns back around, and then it starts: sweet Beatrice, now unexpectedly savage, lays into him:

> Dante, because Virgil has departed
> do not weep, do not weep yet—
> there is another sword to make you weep.[41]

She is aggressive, demanding, and sarcastic, mockingly asking him how he dares to come to this mountain of joy, given that he was adverse to happiness in life.[42] She berates him for having misused his unusually generous set of gifts.[43] Dante describes her words as "sharp,"

---

[36]Dante, *Purgatorio* 29.16-21.

[37]Dante, *Purgatorio* 29.52-53.

[38]Dante, *Purgatorio* 29.73-74.

[39]For more on this, see my *Beginner's Guide to Dante's "Comedy"* (Grand Rapids, MI: Baker Academic, 2018).

[40]Dante, *Purgatorio* 30.31-37.

[41]Dante, *Purgatorio* 28.55-57.

[42]Dante, *Purgatorio* 30.73.

[43]Dante, *Purgatorio* 30.109-17.

"hot," "bitter," and venomous.[44] At one point during this interrogation, Dante lowers his eyes in shame and, doing so, sees his own image on the surface of clear water: "I drew back my eyes."[45] He is too ashamed to bear the sight of his own face. In this amazing and unexpected scene, Dante is emotionally cut, psychologically stung by nettle,[46] and humiliated to the point that he lets flow forth his tears in a great rush of mountain waters coming down in a warm spring:

> the ice that had confined my heart
> was turned to breath and water and in anguish
> flowed from my breath through eyes and mouth.[47]

But the real mystery of the scene is that Dante is made to undergo this interrogation *after* climbing the mountain of purgation, a place which had been created and designed to provide souls a series of spiritual exercises and prayer through which they can pass to be made clean. And Dante went through them all. And so, we can only conclude, that Beatrice's harsh, explosive words are meant to make the pilgrim gaze more inwardly still, to make a deep confession. He must confess his primal guilt: that he willingly abandoned a vision of primordial beauty. Dante must open up the inner sanctum of the heart. At last, under the intense and fiery judgment of Beatrice, the pilgrim is made to repent to the core, and then he is violently baptized and thoroughly cleansed.[48] When he is clean, and only then, Beatrice removes her veil, and her beauty will be so brilliant that Dante will not be able take it all in.[49]

Lewis undertook his first *imitatio*, or recycling and rewriting, of this passage (for *The Great Divorce*) in order to explore what would have happened if a Dante-like figure (in this case the Tragedian) had not come to make a deep confession. The second time Lewis rewrote the

---

[44]Dante, *Purgatorio* 31.3, 30.72, 30.81, 31.75, respectively.
[45]Dante, *Purgatorio* 30.77.
[46]Dante, *Purgatorio* 31.85.
[47]Dante, *Purgatorio* 30.97-99.
[48]Dante, *Purgatorio* 31.94-96.
[49]Dante, *Purgatorio* 32.8.

final canti of *Purgatorio*, though, he did so in order to portray an intensely personal I-Thou moment of unveiling: the judgment of Orual. Over the course of his retelling of Apuleius's Cupid and Psyche myth, Lewis goes out of his way to describe Orual as one who has lived her life in the midst of external things, keeping herself busy with projects and ambitions, so as never to have to face her own vacuous interior. Orual wears a veil the entirety of her life, and the veil functions as a symbol of one who refuses to let her inner self be known, who refuses to unveil herself, even to her own eyes. Against this background of lifelong secrecy and self-deception, the final judgment scene comes as devastatingly intimate. Just as Dante is forced by Beatrice to utter his confession at the end of *Purgatorio*, Orual is forced to let herself be known, to be open, to be vulnerable, to "unveil."

In the final period of her life, Orual comes to be discontent with herself, persuaded that her soul is as cramped and disfigured as her aged body. In light of such self-knowledge, she bravely determines to let go of her hatred and resentment and to "practice philosophy," as her childhood tutor, a Greek (Stoic), taught her to. Alas, her human efforts to bring about inner purity fail, as she laments, "I would set out boldly each morning to be just and calm and wise in all my thoughts and acts; but before they had finished dressing me I would find that I was back . . . in some old rage, resentment, gnawing fantasy, or sullen bitterness. I could not hold out half an hour."[50] Shortly after these failed attempts Orual has a dream, a dream that Lewis is careful to characterize, in medieval fashion, as a "true dream," the same sort of dream Lewis tried to write up in *Great Divorce*.[51] In this dream, Orual has to walk across a desert carrying a scroll in her hand. To her shame and embarrassment, though, she realizes that a great assembly (analogous to the mystical procession that touches down in the Earthly Garden in *Purgatorio* 29) has gathered to listen to her read her scroll, which, unbeknownst to her, is a record of all her subconscious complaints against the gods. Soon Orual, now standing unwillingly

---

[50]C. S. Lewis, *Till We Have Faces: A Myth Retold* (San Francisco: HarperOne, 2017), 282.
[51]See *DI*, 63-64.

in front of a massive assembly (like Dante the pilgrim), as if under a spell, is forced to go on reading her scroll, exposing what she had thought had been kept secret: "It was a great assembly, all staring upon me, and I uplifted on my perch above their heads. Never in peace or war have I seen so vast a concourse. There were ten thousands of them, all silent, every face watching me."[52] When she comes to the end of her complaint, though, she is further humiliated. She can no longer hide from anything: "'Uncover her,' said the judge. Hands came from behind me and tore off my veil—after it, every rag I had on. The old crone . . . stood naked before those countless gazers. No thread to cover me, no bowl in my hand to hold the water of death; only my book."[53]

What is most fascinating about this viscerally-moving scene is that Orual, in a moment of vulnerability and exposure, is made to come to terms with what she is actually angry at. She is made to admit that she had indeed experienced a real encounter with divinity, and she also is made to admit to having made up excuses her whole life, in which she tried to ignore that encounter with the gods, to explain it away. Finally, she must admit that what makes her most angry is that the gods are winsome on account of their fearful beauty. If they were ugly, then it would be easier to hate them; it would be easier to refuse to let go of the small and inferior things we cling to so fiercely, but if they are beautiful, then we have no excuses for, territorially, guarding the boundaries of our hearts. As Orual puts it,

> It would be far better for us if you were foul and ravening. We'd rather you drank their blood than stole their hearts. We'd rather they were ours and dead than yours and made immortal. . . . Why? What should I care for some horrible, new happiness which I hadn't given her and which separated her from me? . . . Did you ever remember whose the girl was? She was mine. *Mine*.[54]

---

[52]Lewis, *Till We Have Faces*, 289.
[53]Lewis, *Till We Have Faces*, 289.
[54]Lewis, *Till We Have Faces*, 290-91.

Orual here references her beloved sister, Psyche, who had to be sacrificed to the gods, but tellingly refers to her as her possession. In his *Letters to Malcolm*, Lewis employs the same potent image of unveiling, in a passage which can cast light on Orual's deep conversion. Lewis asks, "What, then, are we really doing" when we pray? God does not need to be informed about our fears and needs, and given that we "are always completely . . . known to God," what are we actually doing when we express the desires of the heart to God?[55] To answer this, Lewis used the metaphor of unveiling—that is, letting ourselves come to be known by God, letting ourselves come to be in tune with his being. God knows most creatures as "things," such as "earthworms, cabbages, and nebulae." They are

> objects of Divine knowledge. But when we (a) become aware of the fact . . . and (b) ascent with all our will to be so known, then we treat ourselves, in relation to God, not as things but as persons. We have *unveiled*. Not that any *veil* could have baffled His sight. The change is in us. The passive changes to the active. Instead of merely being known, we show, we tell, we offer ourselves to view.[56]

And this is how the judgment scene of *Till We Have Faces* concludes, with Orual being forced to look on the ugliness of her own desire—which she had let herself pretend was noble throughout the entirety of her life. Once she has been unveiled, acknowledging that she herself is in need of love, she can lay aside her self-imposed feeling of achieving virtue exclusively through her own strength. She can let herself be the recipient of love. And so, when Orual finally sees Psyche again, the latter now raised to her full glory, she falls at her feet in tears and confesses, "Oh Psyche, oh goddess. . . . Never again will I call you mine; but all there is of me shall be yours. Alas, you know now what it's worth. I never wished you well, never had one selfless thought of you. I was a craver."[57]

---

[55]Lewis, *Letters to Malcolm*, 20.
[56]Lewis, *Letters to Malcolm*, 21 (emphasis added).
[57]Lewis, *Till We Have Faces*, 305.

But Psyche, repeating words from Lewis's favorite poet, George Herbert, says, "you must stand up . . . Did I not tell you . . . that a day was coming when you and I would meet in my house and no cloud between us?"[58] Orual concludes, "Joy silenced me."[59]

In these powerful concluding words, Lewis gives in fictionalized form his idea of unveiling, that deep confession in which I stop hiding from myself and stop hiding from my God, and come into the full presence of God, who is now a "Thou," encountering divinity in all of its purity and loveliness and mercy, and even fearful intimacy. Only this can wash away our fierce clinging to the small loves of this world, our twisted possessiveness, and can make us clean. But we need the gods to do it for us.

---

[58]Lewis, *Till We Have Faces*, 306.
[59]Lewis, *Till We Have Faces*, 306.

CHAPTER EIGHT

MODERN SCIENCE and MEDIEVAL MYTH

The Relevance of Medieval Cosmology

Atheist: *"You see, the real objection goes far deeper. The whole picture of the universe which science has given us makes it such rot to believe that the Power at the back of it all could be interested in us tiny little creatures crawling about on an unimportant planet! It was all so obviously invented by people who believed in a flat earth with the stars only a mile or two away!"*

Christian: *"When did people believe that?"*

A: *"Why, all those old Christian chaps you're always talking about did. I mean Boethius and Augustine and Thomas Aquinas and Dante."*

C: *"Sorry," said I, "but this is one of the few subjects I do know something about."*

I reached out my hand to a bookshelf. "You see this book," I said, "Ptolemy's Almagest. . . . *Just read that," I said pointing to Book I, chapter 5.*

A: *"The earth,"* read out my friend, hesitating a bit as he translated the Latin, *"the earth, in relation to the distance of the fixed stars, has no appreciable size and must be treated as a mathematical point!"*

There was another short silence.

A: *"Did they really know that* then?*"*

C. S. LEWIS, "RELIGION AND SCIENCE,"
in God in the Dock, 74-75.

ONE OF THE FIERCEST TWENTIETH-CENTURY critics of religion, a man who contemptuously dismissed Christianity as an outdated and archaic religion that the modern scientific world had now outgrown, was a young man by the name of Jack Lewis.[1] In the 1910s, before his famous conversion some two decades later, he mocked Christianity on account of its historical entanglement with the premodern vision of the cosmos. Because Christianity was born into what was still a world of myth, his argument went, it took as its inheritance the imaginative vocabulary of mythology, and because the historical articulation of Christian dogma unfolded within the period during which philosophical system-builders were erecting the medieval model, its theological language, terminology, and debates are shot through with metaphors drawn from the pre-modern cosmos. In this way, Christianity is compromised, tainted, polluted by the literalism of its mythological inheritance and the literalism of the ancient cosmos. And so, Christianity is freighted by—"embarrassed" (in both senses)—the thought-world of the prescientific age, entangled within a "system of names, rituals, and metaphors, which persists" even if we have rejected the ancient cosmology it was based on.[2]

---

[1]See Alister McGrath, *The Intellectual World of C. S. Lewis* (London: Wiley-Blackwell, 2013), 55.
[2]"Myth Became Fact," *EC*, 138.

What the young critic kept secret until a much later date was that at the same time he was espousing his commitment to a world of fact, he was also spending a good deal of time quietly resenting the world he believed in. And like his once-agnostic friend and debating partner, Owen Barfield, he was also experiencing, even suffering, haunting moments of longing and desire for a world that transcended mundane needs or appetites.[3] These two worlds—a world of mere fact and matter, and a world of "quality" (Barfield's term)—could not exist simultaneously, and thus Lewis came to a moment of crisis, which he famously summed up in this way: "The two hemispheres of my mind were in the sharpest contrast. On the one side a many-islanded sea of poetry and myth; on the other a glib and shallow 'rationalism.' Nearly all that I loved I believed to be imaginary; nearly all that I believed to be real I thought grim and meaningless."[4]

And so, part of the process of conversion for Lewis was tied up in discovering an answer to the objections formulated by his former self, the one who had dismissed the mythological imagination as nothing but pleasurable superstition. How could *modern* humans be Christians? In this way, Lewis's own experience of being divided between love of myth and logical conviction with regard to philosophical naturalism gave him the impetus, in his later years, for him to develop his own approach to the "problem of myth." In this chapter, then, I want to take up what I will call Lewis's "epistemological" defense of "Old Western," to be distinguished from his "ethical" justification for Old Western (that is, if we have nothing more than heads our hearts will wither), described in a previous chapter. Indeed, in the "epistemological" defense

---

[3] "Barfield notes that as a young boy he was raised without religious beliefs and if anything a slight bias against them. . . . But as he grew older he noted, 'I began to abhor this vacuum in myself which did not at all fit with the promptings either of my emotional or of my moral nature,'" as cited in Michael Vincent Di Fuccia, *Owen Barfield: Philosophy, Poetry, and Theology* (Eugene, OR: Cascade Books, 2016), 2. For Barfield's influence of Lewis, see also Lionel Adey, *C. S. Lewis's Great War with Owen Barfield* (Wellington, NZ: University of Victoria Press, 1979). Their famous correspondence—which they termed "the Great War"—has been recently edited by Norbert Feinendegen and Arend Smilde in *The "Great War" of Owen Barfield and C. S. Lewis*, special edition of *Inklings Studies Supplement* (Oxford: C. S. Lewis Society, 2015).

[4] *SBJ*, 170.

of the premodern way of thinking (so indebted to Owen Barfield), Lewis developed a way of seeing myth such that it was not a liability for Christianity, but its glory. What is more, his "philosophy of mythology" provided him with a way to explain how modern science and ancient mythology could be reconciled.

THE PROBLEM OF MYTH

Even after he had become a Christian, Lewis continually expressed an initial embarrassment about the literalism that seemed inescapable in certain Christian doctrines. For instance, in his sermon "Transposition," he had to admit that if he encountered a large group of people shouting out gibberish and claiming to speak in mystically incomprehensible languages, he would find the psychologist's explanation of "mass hysteria" plausible.[5] Similarly, he begins "The Weight of Glory" by confessing that imagining the Christian's heavenly reward as some kind of physical luminosity was repellent to his sensibility.[6] And throughout *Letters to Malcolm* Lewis takes modernizing objections to the faith very seriously.[7] In general we find him sympathetic and patient with critics who worry that Christianity's ancient inheritance is a liability, given that its quasi-mythological nature puts it fundamentally at odds with modern scientific thinking, as if Christianity were like a building so old it could not even be retrofitted for modern living. In his remarkable "Dogma and the Universe," Lewis states this suspicion poignantly:

> It is a common reproach against Christianity that its dogmas are unchanging, while human knowledge is in continual growth. Hence, to unbelievers, we seem to be always engaged in the hopeless task of trying to force new knowledge into molds which it has outgrown. . . . It seems clear to [the unbeliever] that, if our

---

[5]C. S. Lewis, "Transposition," in *The Weight of Glory: And Other Addresses* (New York: HarperOne, 1980), 91-92.

[6]Lewis, "The Weight of Glory," 33.

[7]See his comments on Alec Vidler, who wanted a "church with less religion," in "Letter VI," in C. S. Lewis, *Letters to Malcolm: Chiefly on Prayer* (New York: Harvest Books, 1964).

ancestors had known what we know about the universe, Christianity would never have existed at all: and, however we patch and mend, no system of thought which claims to be immutable can, in the long run, adjust itself to our growing knowledge.[8]

It comes as an exhilarating surprise, therefore, to find that Lewis thought Christianity's "mythical" element did *not* disqualify it from being taken seriously in modernity. On the contrary, once we have the clarity and courage to admit that Christianity is indeed a myth, we can go so far as to see this mythological characteristic as Christianity's "most vital and nourishing element."[9] But all of this depends on understanding Lewis's epistemological argument for why we need myth in the first place.

Why can we not, as he puts it in "Myth Became Fact," just dispense with myth, throw away the hull, and keep the kernel of religion? Because every act of thinking is already a metaphorical or mythological act! By this, Lewis meant that anytime we use a term of "value" (that is, any entity whose constitution is not fundamentally material: spirits, virtues, ideas, logic, dogmas, what he calls, in general, "objects of thought"), we are already speaking metaphorically. Anytime I speak about one of these "objects of thought" I am already translating a phenomenon of the mind or heart into a puff of air—a word, in time, physically articulated, and sensuously passed along to my interlocutor. Indeed, words themselves are ineluctably metaphorical: we cannot trade out metaphorically laden words for metaphor-free ones. We can only replace words whose metaphors are still alive for us with words whose metaphors we have now forgotten, but this does not solve the problem:

> We [Christians] are invited [by modern critics] to restate our belief in a form free from metaphor and symbol. The reason why we don't is that we can't. We can, if you like, say "God entered

---

[8]C. S. Lewis, "Dogma and the Universe," in *God in the Dock: Essays on Theology and Ethics*, ed. Walter Hooper (Grand Rapids, MI: Eerdmans, 1970), 38.
[9]"Myth Became Fact," *EC*, 139.

history" instead of saying "God came down to earth." But, of course, "entered" is just as metaphorical as "came down." You have only substituted horizontal or undefined movement for vertical movement. We can make our language duller; we cannot make it less metaphorical. We can make pictures more prosaic; we cannot be less pictorial. Nor are we Christians alone in this disability. . . . All language about things other than physical objects is necessarily metaphorical.[10]

In other words, our speech will always be inadequate, because the spiritual reality toward which we gesture is "higher" than the earthly, sensuous reality, from which we borrow to make up our language. It's the problem of transposition once again.

Even so, does the necessity of using metaphor mean that we have to knowingly embrace a worldview whose scientific facts we *know* to be false? Lewis stated the objection himself: "I have made no serious effort to hide the fact that the old Model delights me as I believe it delighted our ancestors. Few constructions of the imagination seem to me to have combined splendor, sobriety, and coherence in the same degree. It is possible that some readers have long been itching to remind me that it had a serious defect; *it was not true*."[11] How then is it possible to draw anything from a cosmic model that was not *factually* accurate? How can the study of such a system be anything but an archaeological interest in archaic history?

With this question we come to the heart of myth and metaphor. For Lewis the key to appreciating the enduring value of the medieval model is to realize that, although it was not an archaic myth (like the story of Zeus punishing his father, for example), it was still an attempt to describe the physical operations of the cosmos as an "image" or "icon" (or, as we saw in the passage from *The Allegory of Love*, as "sacramental" or "symbolic"). In other words, the medieval model combined the science of its day with a yet-lingering sense for the

---

[10]"Is Theology Poetry?," *EC*, 18.
[11]*DI*, 216 (emphasis added).

metaphorical characteristic of nature itself. The whole model was guided by the intuition that the very order and physical operations of the universe were expressive of an invisible world; "physics" was a subdiscipline of theology. And so, in this way, nature could be thought of as a great metaphor, a sort of physical, palpable, observable, scientific "myth," which itself was a transposition of the invisible into the visible world, at least to the extent the "impoverished" language of the natural, visible world could accommodate the higher.

Strange as it may seem, these thoughts on the nature of Platonic myth, metaphor, and the symbolic (or sacramental or iconic) nature of the cosmos form the background we need in order to understand Lewis's rejoinder to the objection stated above that because the medieval model is not true it is now worthless. Indeed, even modern science, he argues, is compatible with the great model precisely because a new kind of metaphorical element has reentered contemporary philosophy of science's interest in what is called "modeling" and "paradigms." Lewis responded to his own objection—that Christianity was fatally entangled in a web of myth—with a concession followed by a strikingly brilliant argument. "I agree. It was not true," he says, surprising us. "But I would like to end by saying that this charge can no longer have exactly the same sort of weight for us that it would have had in the nineteenth century." In other words, although we cannot deny that we have measured more, and with greater precision, with instruments of finer calibration, and we must admit that we have discovered fundamental forces and properties that our medieval ancestors were ignorant of, it is, nevertheless, the case that the very words "know" and "truth" in the contemporary scientific community have dramatically changed.[12]

The very idea of what science can and cannot do, as well as how science presents us with its conclusions, underwent a transformation in the early twentieth century. In that extraordinary age, light was found to behave as a wave under certain conditions but also, under

---

[12]*DI*, 216.

different experimental conditions, as a series of bundles of energy (particles). What kind of underlying substance light is actually made of, such that it presents as both wave *and* particles, remains elusive. Lewis followed with interest the research of the quantum physicists of his day, who famously found unpredictable eccentricities in the movement of subatomic particles, including the unpredictability of the place of electrons in their orbits. At the same time, clouds of gas are known to follow simple laws that regulate the relationship between their heat and the pressure they exert on the walls that contain them, but at the molecular level the individual units buzzing around are incomprehensibly complex. We can pose questions about the simple, underlying levels of reality and get answers with predictive power, but our answers do not help us get at the essence of what's happening at the deeper levels. Our observations make up mere "models." In this way, for Lewis, the paradigm-building of contemporary physicists, who teach the curvature of space and the erratic nature of subatomic movements, has unexpected similarities with the medieval mystic, who paradoxically asserted things like, "God is a circle whose center is everywhere and whose circumference is nowhere," as Alan of Lille put it.

In this way, both the medieval mystic and the modern physicist hint, gesture, suggest at what is beyond ordinary thinking. The modern physicist believes that the closest we can get to the "real thing" is mathematical approximations. Everything else is merely an analogy. In this way, Lewis contested, modern scientists have returned to using "parables," being unable to speak about ultimate reality apart from making "models." It was from modern physicists, then, that Lewis borrowed the term, "Model," which he used to refer to the medieval cosmic imaginary. But, he insisted, it would be a mistake to think of these as smaller reduplications such as scaled-down model ships or airplanes. Rather, the model of the physicist (as well as the medieval theologian) merely "suggests." It does not represent.[13]

---

[13]*DI*, 218.

The similarity, then, is found not so much in the "content" of the beliefs, but in the shared conviction that our mental models are but metaphorical pictures. Given that there is a gap between the facts we can know, the facts that make up a model, and ultimate reality, all models are to a certain extent like maps with contour lines, useful for general orientation but not reduplications of the real world: "In going beyond the contour lines . . . he is (if he knows how to read a map) getting nearer to the reality."[14] In this way, Lewis was adamant that, despite his admiration, he was not recommending "a return to the Medieval Model"; rather, he wished to suggest "considerations that may induce us to regard all Models in the right way, respecting each and idolizing none. . . . No Model is a catalogue of ultimate realities, and none is a mere fantasy. Each is a serious attempt to get in all the phenomena known at a given period, and each succeeds in getting in a great many."[15]

HUBBLE . . . AND BERNARD SILVESTRIS?
THE WEIRDNESS OF THE UNIVERSE

This is the first response to the modern suspicion that, because the medieval view of the cosmos is not true, it must be worthless. But Lewis had a second insight into how the medieval model anticipated contemporary science: both modern cosmology and the medieval picture, perhaps surprisingly, share the same attitude regarding the peripheral location of human beings in the dazzlingly strange, grand, and varied universe we inhabit. Indeed, the single most characteristic feature that separates twentieth-century cosmology from its "classic" (eighteenth- and nineteenth-century) formulation is the size and strangeness of the universe, fueled by a series of paradigm-breaking discoveries, which have forced philosophers and scientists to reconceptualize, by orders of magnitude, the size, speed of expansion, and age of the cosmos. For instance, in Hubble's day, there was still debate over exactly what those cloudy nebulae actually were. A leading theory

---

[14]*DI*, 217.
[15]*DI*, 222.

held that nebulae were solar systems in progress, being cooked up in a kind of cosmic oven. The contemporary model of the cosmos, then, was of one great galaxy, with stars and solar systems in various stages of evolution. Hubble, however, had access to a newly built telescope at Mount Wilson, which was at the time the largest in the world. He turned it toward a series of nebulae, including the Andromeda nebula. He was able to resolve the vague, dusty appearance into specific stars, as well as identify within these nebulae stars that periodically pulse in their brightness, called cepheids. Because the rate at which cepheids pulse is related to their absolute brightness, Hubble was able to use them as great cosmic yardsticks, showing that these nebulae were clusters of stars at tremendous distances, whole worlds, infinitely remote. We look out, then, and find "island universes," as large or larger than our own. It was an extraordinary discovery, which forced a recalibration of the size of the universe. The universe turned out to be not only larger than expected but also accelerating, expanding at mind-boggling speeds. "In one fell swoop the visible universe was enlarged by an inconceivable factor, eventually trillions of times over," as Marcia Bartusiak puts it. It was as if "we had been confined to one square yard of Earth's surface, only to suddenly realize that there were now vast oceans and continents, cities and villages, mountains and deserts, previously unexplored and unanticipated."[16]

And since Hubble, the universe has only grown stranger: physicists claim to have discovered the afterglow of the big bang in cosmic background radiation. They have discovered that there are gravitational waves. They have discovered stars that, despite having the same mass as two of our suns, have radii that are only about six miles long, because their cores have collapsed in on themselves during a supernova (neutron stars). And we know that some portions of the universe are so dense that light cannot escape their gravitational field (black holes). We have a cosmos with what seems like an infinite array of cosmological objects, spread out through infinite space, and moving at

---

[16]Marcia Bartusiak, *The Day We Found the Universe* (New York: Pantheon, 2009), xi.

inconceivable speeds: a world of deep time, deep space, dark matter, dark energy, spiral nebulae, and antimatter.

In the popular imagination, these discoveries of modern cosmology have dealt a fatal blow to the alleged ancient conviction that human beings occupy a special part of the universe. We have moved from a universe in which the Sun revolves around the Earth, to a universe in which an Earth revolves around the Sun, to a universe made up of "island universes." But, as Lewis emphasized in almost everything he wrote on the subject, the idea that these shifts in understanding somehow invalidate religious belief is a completely mistaken interpretation of the medieval world itself. In an imagined dialogue published in 1945 (cited as the epigraph to this chapter), Lewis pointed out that premodern cosmographers already described the earth as but a mathematical point with respect to the rest of the universe. Indeed, it was not just that the medieval model was larger than we might expect, but medieval natural philosophers had a kind of universe-centric awe for the cosmos, an attitude Lewis captured in the coinage the "anthropoperipheral" universe—that is, humankind is at the periphery of everything that really matters. This "geocentric universe [was] not in the least anthropocentric,"[17] because it "made man a marginal—almost . . . a suburban—creature."[18] It was not only that "everyone" knew "the Earth is infinitesimally small by cosmic standards"[19] but also that the Earth was made out of the dregs, after the purer bodies of stars had been made (a curious agreement with modern speculation!). Everything interesting, festive, fiery, light, clean, and harmonious was way out *there*, while we, poor fools, dwell at "the lowest point" of the universe, "plunged . . . in unending cold"; the earth was "in fact the 'offscourings of creation,' the cosmic dust-bin,"[20] "'the worst and deadest part of the universe,' 'the lowest story of the house,' the point at which all light, heat, and

---

[17]*DI*, 55.
[18]*DI*, 49.
[19]*DI*, 54.
[20]*DI*, 63.

movement descending from the nobler spheres finally died out into darkness, coldness, and passivity."[21] As we have seen, this is what Lewis called our "anthropoperipheral" position in the cosmos, where, from a great distance, like spectators who didn't get into the stadium, we watch, struggling to hear a sound or catch a glimpse of that distant excitement.[22]

Here, too, Lewis used his fiction to explore such a world from within—the view "along the beam"—using Ransom's captivity on the spaceship in *Out of the Silent Planet* as a way to provide a "point-of-view shot" of what it would have felt like to be immersed in the medieval heavens. In the spaceship, Ransom lies "for hours in contemplation of the skylight. . . . The stars, thick as daisies on an uncut lawn, reigned perpetually with no cloud, no moon, no sunrise to dispute their sway. There were planets of unbelievable majesty, and constellations undreamed of: there were celestial sapphires, rubies, emeralds, and pinpricks of burning gold."[23] The experience of space is so invigorating that Ransom needs no more than a couple of hours of sleep, and he cannot even feel fear, given that the "adventure was too high, its circumstance too solemn, for any emotion save severe delight."[24] Ransom can only smile contentedly that modern science has vindicated the old books: "Stretched naked on his bed, a second Danaë, he found it night by night more difficult to disbelieve in old astrology."[25] He lies in the light "totally immersed in a bath of pure ethereal color and of unrelenting though unwounding brightness."[26]

The medieval cosmos was composed not only of heavens that were steeped in light and energy—dancing and singing and tingling with vibrant joy—but also of intelligent creatures of every variety. Whether

---

[21]C. S. Lewis, *English Literature in the Sixteenth Century* (Oxford: Oxford University Press, 1954), 3.

[22]*DI*, 58.

[23]C. S. Lewis, *Out of the Silent Planet* (New York: Scribner, 2003), 33.

[24]Lewis, *Out of the Silent Planet*, 33.

[25]Lewis, *Out of the Silent Planet*, 33.

[26]Lewis, *Out of the Silent Planet*, 34. See Michael Ward's comments on this passage, *Planet Narnia*, 24-26.

the daimons found in learned accounts or the fairies of popular accounts, the world was full of airy spirits, as well as astral intelligences
and other types of *longaevi*—all reasoning creatures, all with different
bodies made up of varying substances, all of whom possessed reason
and desire. The world was full of living marvels and embodied miracles,
most of which desired no relationship at all with human beings. In some
ways, these creatures of the imagination were much more "at home" in
the enchanted world than human beings.

Being more like the enchanted world, they were better able to dwell
in it as their natural habitat, more "local" in a world of spiritual mystery.
Here again, Lewis was vigilant against the modern tendency to make
spiritual realities more ghostly, less real, less substantial. Rather, when
we call them "supernatural" we should think of them as hyper-natural:
"stronger, more reckless, less inhibited, more triumphantly and imper-
tinently passionate." They are not enslaved to the nutritional needs of
the body, and thus they are free from "responsibilities, shames, scruples,
and melancholy of Man."[27] And in addition to these "long-lived creatures" (*Longaevi*) there were also planets with personalities, stars that
were not inorganic but had "life and intelligence,"[28] and a great cosmic
intellect whose contemplation turned the drive shaft of the world, the
primum mobile.[29]

This feature of the medieval universe also left its mark on Lewis's
imaginative worlds. Narnia, for instance, is populated by all kinds of
races, from centaurs to unicorns to the varied creature that make up
Peter's army in "What Happened About the Statues," in *The Lion, the
Witch and the Wardrobe*. Similarly, "sylvans" and "dryads" populate the
woods of *Prince Caspian* (see "What Lucy Saw"), the fairy-like citizens
haunt the sea in *Voyage of the* Dawn Treader (see "The Wonders of the
Last Sea"), and the dwarf-like creatures burrow leagues underground
in *The Silver Chair* (see "The Disappearance of Jill"). And, yes, there
are stars with intelligence:

---

[27]*DI*, 133-34.
[28]*DI*, 93.
[29]*DI*, 96.

"I am Ramandu. But I see that you stare at one another and have not heard this name. And no wonder, for the days when I was a star had long ceased before any of you knew this world, and all the constellations have changed. . . ."

"In our world," said Eustace, "a star is a huge ball of flaming gas."

"Even in your world, my son, that is not what a star is but only what it is made of."[30]

Similarly, in the learned literature of the medieval period, Latin-writing poets like Bernard Silvestris and Alan of Lille invented poems of medieval space travel, in which they imagined astral journeys where all these mysterious cosmic forces were met and conversed with. The *Cosmographia*, for example, is an exceedingly strange, allegorical work that renders the science of antiquity into an artful allegory. Like Boethius's *Consolation*, it is a *prosimetrum*, which means it alternates between baroquely ornate Latin prose and poems that imitate classical meters. Bernard's poem begins with a description of the creation of the world (by Nous, which is the classicizing "intellect" of God) and ends with a discussion of the creation of the human being by a trio of cosmic forces (allegorized as goddesses): Nature, Urania (the Queen of the Stars), and Physis (the ruler of biological life). In the middle portion of the work, Nous orders Nature to travel through the various heavens to seek out Urania. So Natura leaves Earth behind, travels upward through the heavens, and is continuously "dazzled" and left with "blinking eyes," as she takes in the bizarre universe piece by piece.[31] First she comes to the region of Anastros, a region on the border of air and ether, with a "light unwavering, its calm perpetual."[32] Then she travels along the Zodiac, and sees a "numberless throng, a mob of souls clustered about the boundary of Cancer."[33] Later she learns that this dense cluster of spirits is waiting to be sewed into the

---

[30]C. S. Lewis, *The Voyage of the* Dawn Treader (New York: HarperCollins, 1984), 208-9.

[31]Bernard Silvestris, *Cosmographia* 2.3.12. For text see Bernardus Silvestris, *Poetic Works*, trans. Winthrop Wetherbee, Dumbarton Oaks Library (Cambridge, MA: Harvard University Press, 2015).

[32]Silvestris, *Cosmographia* 2.3.5.

[33]Silvestris, *Cosmographia* 2.3.7.

various regions of the world: some are human souls, some will be heavenly angels, some will be "aerial" spirits, some will be aerial spirits that hover close to the earth, and some will be Telluri, "spirits who dwell on earth ... rejoicing now in green hill and flowery mountainside, now in rivers, now clothed in woodland greenery, there Silvans, Pans, and Nerei."[34] All of these lower spirits are overseen by the "Plutonian Usiarch," whose name is Summanus. This is just the beginning of her journey, on which she also meets other Usiarchs, different personalities that rule over various planets. Nature also comes to the outermost circle of the world, ruled by Pantomorphos, who is responsible for all shapes of all creaturely beings.[35] After finding Urania, she accompanies the goddess up to the "realm of pure and uncontaminated light ... the secret abode of supreme and superessential God,"[36] before descending together to Gramision, a sacred spot on earth where the human soul and body will be made.[37] Just as Lewis rewrote Boethius and Plato in *The Last Battle*, rewrote Dante in *The Great Divorce*, and rewrote the philosopher Nicholas of Cusa in the form of a lyric poem (see his "On a Theme from Nicholas of Cusa"), so he transformed Natura's unquestionably strange journey to find Urania into Ransom's journey to visit intelligent astral races. The narrator concludes *Out of the Silent Planet* with a description of the letter that solicited Ransom's story: "I am now working at the Platonists of the twelfth century and incidentally discovering that they wrote damnably difficult Latin. In one of them, Bernardus Silvestris, there is a word I should particularly like your views on—the word *Oyarses*."

On a deeper level, Bernard Silvestris didn't just provide Lewis with a plot in need of updating; rather, he, and the whole premodern tradition (from *Job* through the Platonic tradition), turned out to be surprisingly relevant. Their worlds shared fundamental properties with the cosmos of Arthur Edington and Edwin Hubble. For both

---

[34]Silvestris, *Cosmographia* 2.7.11.
[35]Silvestris, *Cosmographia* 2.3.9.
[36]Silvestris, *Cosmographia* 2.5.2.
[37]Silvestris, *Cosmographia* 2.9.2.

medievals and moderns, mysterious entities, hardly understood, emerge out of darkness and present themselves to rapt human observers. For modern cosmologists, as stated above, the universe is packed full of marvels and strange entities. But for every spiral nebula, black hole, and neutron star, we can find a corresponding Pantomorphos, Urania, and Gramision in the old authors. In both the medieval and modern worlds, human beings are privileged observers of the great cosmic dance, even if they are not the central participants.

In this way the anthropoperipheral of medieval cosmology has an unexpected similarity with the modern cosmology. Viewed in the right way they both can be seen in a religious and poetic sense, and for the same reasons. The universe as understood in modern cosmology is, too, a great cosmic symphony—or, as Lewis adds in language that echoes his description of the Platonic universe, a "shadow of an image of God":

> We are inveterate poets. When a quantity is very great, we cease to regard it as mere quantity. Our imaginations awake. Instead of mere quantity, we now have a quality—the sublime. . . . When we are frightened by the greatness of the universe, we are (almost literally) frightened by our own shadows; for these light years and billions of centuries are as arithmetic until the shadow of man, the poet, the maker of myth, falls upon them. . . . To puny man, the great nebula in Andromeda owes in a sense its greatness . . . I hope you do not think I am suggesting that God made the spiritual nebulae solely or chiefly in order to give me the experience of awe and bewilderment. I have not the faintest idea why He made them; on the whole, I think it would be rather surprising if I had. As far as I understand the matter, Christianity is not wedded to an anthropocentric view of the universe as a whole.[38]

This meditation on the anthropoperipheral cosmos led Lewis to some of his most daring and provocative, medieval-inspired thought experiments: the possibility that there are multiple intelligent races, spread throughout the universe, all at different stages in their own

---

[38]Lewis, "Dogma and the Universe," 41-42.

salvation stories![39] In his *Ransom Trilogy*, Lewis pictures life on Mars and life on Venus, each occupied by different intelligent, nonhuman species, but whose salvation story is playing out differently. Similarly, in *The Magician's Nephew*, we find Lewis's world between worlds, a central hub of portals that gives access to innumerable worlds at different stages in their development: the world of Jadis, already shriveled up and at its end; Narnia, coming into being; and our world, presently lost in the middle of its quotidian struggle to choose real good over evil. What comes as a surprise is how seriously Lewis took the hypothesis. In his nonfiction apologetical work (such as "Dogma and the Universe" but also in *Miracles*), we find him repeatedly setting forward speculations that effectively reprise the cosmic world of Bernard Silvestris, now dressed in the garb of modern physics and sci-fi:

> It is, of course, the essence of Christianity that God loves man and for his sake became man and died. But that does not prove that man is the sole end of Nature. In the parable (Matthew 18:12; Luke 15:4), it was the one last sheep that the shepherd went in search of: it was not the only sheep in the flock, and we are told that it was not the most valuable—save in so far as the most desperately in need has, while the need lasts, a peculiar value in the eyes of Love. The doctrine of the Incarnation would conflict with what we know of this vast universe only if we knew also that there were other rational species in it who had, like us, fallen, and who need redemption in the same mode, and that they had not been vouchsafed it. But we know none of these things. It may be full of life that needs no redemption. It may be full of life that has been redeemed. It may be full of things quite other than life which satisfy the Divine Wisdom in fashions one cannot conceive.[40]

The genius of all this is that even if such a multiuniverse reality were true—in which we human beings are just one of many intelligent races, on the periphery of our own universe, living out our own version of

---

[39]See his 1958 letter to Mrs. Hook (*Letters*, 3:1004).
[40]Lewis, "Dogma and the Universe," 43.

the salvation story—this does not mean we are unimportant. In Lewis's imagination, we have to remember that it is Aslan who is judge; Aslan who is maker; Aslan who is quietly whispering to souls. In this way, every race, however peripheral, is at the center of its Creator's affection. In fact, Lewis goes even further, imagining a world in which every atom exists as if it were the only object of the Father's affection:

> If there is a Providence at all, everything is providential and every providence is a special providence. It is an old and pious saying that Christ died not only for Man but for each man, just as much as if each had had been the only man there was. Can I not believe the same of this creative act—which, as spread out in time, we call destiny or history? It is for the sake of each human soul. Each is an end. Perhaps for each beast. Perhaps even each particle of matter—the night sky suggests that the inanimate also has for God some value we cannot imagine. His ways are not (not there, anyway) like ours. . . .
>
> One of the purposes for which God instituted prayer may have been to bear witness that the course of events is not governed like a state but created like a work of art to which every being makes its contribution and (in prayer) a conscious contribution, and in which every being is both an end and a means. . . . The great work of art was made for the sake of all it does and is, down to the curve of every wave and the flight of every insect.[41]

From this perspective the incarnation regains its sense of astonishment and stupefaction. If we are really a marginal race on the edge of a mediocre galaxy, rotating around an average star, the fact that the Creator decided to come to our race, dwell with us, spend time talking to socially unimportant people in the heat of the afternoon, is all the more glorious. He is, after all, the one for whom, as Lewis might have put it, spiral nebulae swirl and black holes hide behind their gravitational veils.

---

[41]C. S. Lewis, *Letters to Malcolm: Chiefly on Prayer* (New York: Harvest Books, 1964), 55-56.

CONCLUSION

NOSTALGIA *for* *the* FUTURE

ONCE, QUOTING WORDSWORTH'S "I'd rather be a pagan / suckled in a creed outworn," Lewis, hardly joking, asserted that if he had to choose between living among "Western, mechanized, democratic, secularized men" he would almost rather

> listen to the drum-beat in my blood . . . and join in the song of the Maenads:

> *Happy they whom the Daimons*
> *Have befriended, who have entered*
> *The divine orgies, making holy*
> *Their life-days, till the dance throbs*
> *In their heart-beats, while they romp with*
> *Dionysus on the mountains . . .*
> Yes, almost . . .[1]

When comparing the drab, modern, mechanistic world in which humans are the only intelligent agents to a world of paganism, charged with spirituality, under pressure, as it were, threatening to erupt out of the ground with irrational and exuberant joy, Lewis leaned toward the

---

[1]"Religion Without Dogma?," *EC*, 175.

pagan. Contrast such premodern visions of exuberant joy with how Lewis described the dolorous piety of modern religion, what he called a "minimal religion" which has "nothing that can convince, convert, or (in the higher sense) console: nothing, therefore, which can restore vitality to our civilization. It is not costly enough."[2] It is, seemingly, for this reason that Bacchus keeps making unexpected appearances throughout the Narnia books.[3] Bacchus is the liberator, the joy-bringer, the mirth-maker, and he shatters our frigid paradigms of religion when they become nothing more than being nice and respectable and socially responsible: "Bacchus and the Maenads—his fierce, madcap girls—and Silenus were still with them. . . . Everyone was awake, everyone was laughing, flutes were playing, cymbals clashing. Animals . . . were crowding upon them from every direction."[4]

Nostalgia for this world of wild and disorienting joy was probably the chief sentiment of Lewis and his friends the Inklings throughout their lives. They repeatedly confessed to experiencing such nostalgia while reading ancient texts. But what they always insisted on—and this is where some of Tolkien and Lewis's more vindictive critics miss the point—was that the nostalgia they experienced was not just sentimentality for a past age. Rather, as Tolkien so enigmatically put it, it was a hunger for a "remoteness" even "older" than antiquity. Fairy stories, Tolkien said, "are now *old*, and antiquity has an appeal in itself. . . . And yet always the chief flavor of [these tales] in the memory [is] . . . distance and a great abyss of time, not measurable even by *twe tusend Johr*. . . . [They] open a door on Other Time, and if we pass through, though only for a moment, we stand outside our own time, outside Time itself, maybe."[5] Lewis echoes Tolkien's words, in describing a longing "almost like heartbreak, the memory of Joy itself, the knowledge that I had once had what I had now lacked for years,

---

[2]"Religion Without Dogma?," *EC*, 175.

[3]For example, C. S. Lewis, *The Lion, the Witch and the Wardrobe* (New York: HarperCollins, 1984), 16.

[4]C. S. Lewis, *Prince Caspian* (New York: HarperCollins, 1984), 215.

[5]"On Fairy-Stories," *Essays Presented to Charles Williams*, ed. C. S. Lewis (Oxford: Oxford University Press, 1947), 57.

that I was returning at last from exile and desert lands to my own country."[6] But this desire for this distant country should not be conflated with what is merely old; that "Other Time" merely uses the literature of the past as a medium. The past cannot be the object of nostalgia itself. In other words, nostalgia—viewed rightly— metamorphosizes into hope.

In *Miracles*, Lewis quite bluntly says we suffer from a lack of hope. Our diluted conception of heaven is connected to "the fact that the specifically Christian virtue of Hope has in our time grown so languid," whereas "our fathers, peering into the future saw gleams of gold."[7] When we think about the beliefs of the old world—say, how Roland could not break his sword because it had become "enchanted" with holiness, or how Saint Benedict caused clay vessels bearing poison to crack when he blessed them—we are entertained, but feel a little uneasy. In modernity it is often the case that the "bodily" and the "spiritual" don't go together well. And for this reason, Lewis thought that "probably every Christian now alive finds a difficulty in recon- ciling the two things he has been told about heaven—that it is . . . a life in Christ, a vision of God, a ceaseless adoration, and that it is, on the other hand, a bodily life. When we seem nearest to the vision of God in this life, the body seems almost an irrelevance."[8] But he also insisted that this sublimation of the bodily, this marriage of the material and the spiritual, is what is to come:

> It is not an accident that simple-minded people [in the archaic age] . . . should blend the ideas of God and Heaven and the blue sky. It is a fact, not a fiction, that light and life-giving heat do come down from the sky to Earth. The analogy of the sky's role to begetting and of the Earth's role to bearing is sound. . . . The huge dome of the sky is of all things sensuously perceived the most like infinity. And when God made space and worlds that move in space, and clothed our world with air, and gave us such

[6]*SBJ*, 73.
[7]C. S. Lewis, *Miracles* (San Francisco: HarperSanFrancisco, 2001), 265.
[8]Lewis, *Miracles*, 259.

eyes and such imaginations as we have, He knew what the sky would mean to us.[9]

In other words, it is no accident that the physical world evoked spiritual responses from archaic man. The world was designed to elicit these just sentiments, which had been, if you will, programmed within. The professor of medieval literature believed that we have to own the modernity of our sentiments, our sense of "exile" from the past and from the enchanted cosmos; we can't falsify our emotions, pretending we see and feel as those in an older age would have felt. Nevertheless, the great lover of myth desperately wanted to acknowledge that primitive human beings had got hold of some deep truth, which is not out of date: "The archaic type of thought which could not clearly distinguish spiritual 'Heaven' from the sky, is from our point of view a confused type of thought. But it also resembles and anticipates a type of thought which will one day be true. That archaic sort of thinking will become simply the correct sort when Nature and Spirit are fully harmonized."[10]

In the grand historical scheme, then, modern estrangement, brought on by the necessity to pass through the era after the Great Divide, is a paradoxical gift. By being forced to wake up to the fact that the old model was not fully correct, we are deprived of the consolation of resting in the merely natural world. The positive result of our exile is our painful sense of loss and longing, which speaks to a desire, not just to see beauty, but to be beauty. In "The Weight of Glory," Lewis describes this very desire. Sometimes when we look on beauty, we are sad when we realize that "we have been mere spectators. Beauty has smiled, but not to welcome us; her face was turned in our direction, but not to see us." This experience of alienation, however, comes as an extraordinary stimulus to hope:

> Apparently, then, our lifelong nostalgia, our longing to be reunited with something in the universe from which we now feel cut off, to be on the inside of some door which we have always

---

[9]Lewis, *Miracles*, 258.
[10]Lewis, *Miracles*, 262.

seen from the outside, is no mere neurotic fancy, but the truest index of our real situation. . . . In one way, of course, God has given us the Morning Star already: you can go and enjoy the gift on many fine mornings if you get up early enough. What more, you may ask, do we want? Ah, but we want so much more. . . . The poets and the mythologies know all about it. We do not want merely to see beauty. . . . We want something else which can hardly be put into words—to be united with the beauty we see, to bathe in it, to become part of it. That is why we have peopled air and earth and water with gods and goddesses and nymphs and elves. . . . That is why the poets tell us such lovely falsehoods.[11]

In the age of exile—modernity—we don't have the option of resting in an enchanted landscape, and this helps reveal to us, again, that our deepest desire is not just to witness beauty but to hold it within. Without exile, we might have been contented with too little. Thus the sentiment of nostalgia we get from reading books from the past is not necessarily misplaced, provided we understand that they are merely symptoms of a greater longing for something that has not yet come.

In "Miracles of the New Creation," toward the end of *Miracles*, Lewis suggests that the resurrection has been misunderstood; it was not just another miracle, but rather the first of a new type of miracle. So many other miracles were just the short-circuiting of a natural process: when Christ turned water into wine, he was doing quickly what nature does every season in an annual biological miracle. The same could be said for healing. Christ healing the sick was, if you will, a more dramatic way of bringing health to an ailing body, but not a qualitatively different experience from when I find myself healing from a wound or recovering from an illness. But the resurrection was the first miracle of a new age—that is, the beginning of a great reversal. Christ's resurrection, Lewis insists, is a wholly new chapter in the world, an opening of a door that had been previously locked. Whereas moderns tend to think of the resurrection as

---

[11]*EC*, 104. This passage pairs well with his description, in *SBJ*, of the "ravenous desire to break the bounds, to tear the curtain, to be in the secret" (177).

important, because of its proof value (if we know it happened, then we can prove Jesus Christ's divinity), Lewis argues forcefully that this misses the greatest part of the miracle. It is not just some proof to win an argument, but the first act of drawing all of creation up to a new level of dignity. Moreover, it was the first act in refashioning space and time itself, as well as the relationship between mind and matter. This leads Lewis to make some bold speculations, which make us see that the wild fantasy in his space stories and Narnian tales were not "mere" fantasy. Lewis wonders if in the new creation our minds will be able to control the matter around them, just as now our minds extend their authority throughout our bodies. If such a thing were ever to happen, then we would be the beneficiaries of something akin to magic, except without the lust for power. In this way, the model, despite some of its factual inaccuracies, had something deeply (psychologically) true at its core: a longing for the obliteration of the distinction between the spiritual realm and material; or, to state it positively, a desire for a world in which God shows himself forth in the visible world and in which our own minds can incarnate themselves in the world around us. Lewis was nostalgic for the future. The old model was not wrong, strictly speaking, but a kind of deep, human subconscious desire for a world that, in some sense, we are meant to occupy, but not yet.

I would like to conclude, then, with similar words from Tolkien, who recalled how every good fairy tale has an intensely happy ending, one that can "give to child or man that hears it . . . a catch of the breath, a beat and lifting of the heart, near to (or indeed accompanied by) tears."[12] But in the best fairy tales, the happy ending is so unexpected ("never to be counted on to recur"[13]) that the experience could be described as "catastrophically good," a "Eucatastrophe," which provides us with "a fleeting glimpse of Joy, Joy beyond the walls of the world, poignant as grief."[14] Tolkien concludes his famous essay by reminding us that this is exactly our situation:

---

[12] *Tolkien: On Fairy Stories,* ed. Verlyn Flieger and Douglas Anderson (London: Harper-Collins, 2008), 75.

[13] Tolkien, "On Fairy-Stories," 243.

[14] Tolkien, "On Fairy-Stories," 75.

It is not difficult to imagine the peculiar excitement and joy that one would feel, if any specially beautiful fairy-story were found to be "primarily" true, its narrative to be history. . . . This joy would have exactly the same quality, if not the same degree, as the joy which the "turn" in a fairy-story gives: such joy has the very taste of primary truth. . . . It looks forward (or backward: the direction in this regard is unimportant) to the Great Eucatastrophe. . . . Art has been verified.[15]

The experience of nostalgia is a feeling of beauty's remoteness, but only because it is so far in the future, rooted "deep down things." It is hope. And the great thing about true hope, this nostalgia for the future, is that it has none of the irritability, fear, anxiety, and discouragement that flavors many of the words of those who describe the demise of Christendom in our day. We were denied the garden, and then we were exiled from the enchanted cosmos. Now we must own our modernity. But by doing so, we engage in an extraordinary ascesis of the senses. We must move forward and look beyond.

---

[15]Tolkien, "On Fairy-Stories," 78.

INDEX